REMEMBERING OLD JAMESTOWN

A Look Back at the Other South

MARY A. BROWNING

THE History PRESS

Published by The History Press
Charleston, SC 29403
www.historypress.net

First published 2008

Manufactured in the United States

ISBN 978.1.59629.591.9

Library of Congress Cataloging-in-Publication Data

Browning, Mary A.
Remembering Old Jamestown : a look back at the other South / Mary A. Browning.
p. cm.
Includes bibliographical references and index.
ISBN 978-1-59629-591-9
1. Jamestown (N.C.)--History--Anecdotes. 2. Jamestown (N.C.)--Social life and customs--Anecdotes. 3. Jamestown (N.C.)--Biography--Anecdotes. 4. Historic buildings--North Carolina--Jamestown. 5. Historic sites--North Carolina--Jamestown. 6. Jamestown (N.C.)--Buildings, structures, etc. I. Title.
F264.J355B765 2008
975.6'62--dc22

2008041953

Notice: The information in this book is true and complete to the best of our knowledge. It is offered without guarantee on the part of the author or The History Press. The author and The History Press disclaim all liability in connection with the use of this book.

REMEMBERING OLD JAMESTOWN

CONTENTS

Part I

Quaker Life

Quakers were the first settlers in Jamestown in the 1750s, and for many years theirs was the dominant influence in this settlement along the upper Deep River.

James Mendenhall House and Mills

If there is one place in Jamestown that should be commemorated with a sign showing its historic importance, it is the location of James Mendenhall's mill and house—even if it is officially in High Point now.

Jamestown was named for James Mendenhall, a Quaker from Chester County, Pennsylvania, who moved to then Rowan County, North Carolina, in 1759, according to his descendants (by 1762, according to documentary evidence). His wife, Hannah Thomas, and six of his eight children came with him, and he took up a grant of land from colonial proprietor John Earl Granville for 204 acres adjoining Richard Beeson on Deep River. He was, at that time, forty-four years old. In 1775, James left his house and mill in the capable hands of his son George Mendenhall, and moved on to Georgia, where he died in 1781. It was George who developed the plan for the village named Jamestown, and who left town lots to his children in his will.

The house and mills that James and his sons built have been gone for about seventy-five years, the foundations drowned by the waters of High Point City Lake.

The house was built on the south bank of what was then the shallow West Fork of Deep River, near the western edge of James's grant. At the time, the river probably could be crossed on a foot log by a pedestrian or easily forded by horse or wagon. This house site is well known, just east of and a stone's throw from the present bridge on Penny Road.

The house had a chimney stone dated 1765 that was rescued in 1929 from the rising lake waters by Martha Robbins Tilden and her daughter, Sophie

Tilden, when the dam was built and the house was demolished. The two diminutive women carried, pushed and rolled the stone from the shore of the lake to their home on Main Street, and of course it was uphill all the way. The cornerstone now rests on a granite windowsill in the 1811 house that James's grandson, Richard Mendenhall, built in Jamestown.

Another dated stone from the old house is carved with the initials "G.C.M." and dated 1843, placed there by James's grandson, George C. Mendenhall, who followed his father, George, as the third generation to live in the house and mind the mills. George C. was responsible for one of the additions to the house. He was a successful lawyer and state legislator.

During the winter of 1999, when the lake water was extremely low, the foundations of the house could be seen, and walked upon if one didn't mind muddy shoes. Photos of the house as it was in the last quarter of the nineteenth century show three distinct buildings attached end-to-end. Unseen behind the house was the river, and the ground in front rose up sharply to discourage building additions in that direction. During his residency, George C. called the house Champlain.

The James Mendenhall House was begun in 1765 and demolished in 1928, when Deep River was dammed nearby to form High Point City Lake. *Courtesy High Point Museum, High Point, North Carolina.*

The mills—a gristmill and a sawmill—were upstream from the house. Some years ago, local residents remembered a milldam west of the present bridge, on the south-curving portion of the river. The original gristmill would have been a tub mill, not the picturesque overshot water wheel that came later. For the curious, a drawing of a typical tub mill of that period can be found in the book *Frontier Living*, by Edwin Tunis.

George C. took seriously his father's will, which charged him to "keep the mills repaired." In 1832, he had them completely rebuilt. According to a 1937 newspaper account, there was a ten-foot-high rock foundation that was three feet thick, where the driving machinery rested. There were three stories above this base, framed in oak and weatherboarded with heart pine cut at the sawmill a few feet up the millrace. The machinery was driven by two overshot water wheels eighteen feet high.

George C. Mendenhall died in an accident while traveling in 1860. Following the 1881 death of his widow, Delphina Gardner Mendenhall, the mill is said to have belonged to Paris Benbow, and then his son Oliver C. Benbow, who in 1902, following a fire, rebuilt the mill on the old foundation. He sold to O.W. Williard, who sold to Sam Stafford, who then sold to Ralto Horney. The property was finally acquired by the City of High Point. Now, the house and mill site is covered by about thirty feet of water, give or take.

Pacifists Face Redcoats

If, the speaker said, magic could transport us back to March 14, 1781, we would be sitting in the old log meetinghouse, looking out the windows at British soldiers camped around the building.

The speaker was the late Algie I. Newlin, the place was Deep River Meeting and his audience was composed mostly of members of Deep River Friends Meeting. The occasion was a 1975 anniversary celebration of the "new" (1875) meetinghouse.

The irony of soldiers camped in the midst of pacifist Quakers was lost on no one.

Newlin's device, imagining the past, is used by many people in this area during the days in early March that led all those years ago to the Battle at Guilford Courthouse, as we try to envision those events.

The increasingly hungry British troops of General Cornwallis's army in 1781 were far from their supply point at Wilmington, and had been ordered to scour the countryside as they moved through the southern part of Guilford County in search of anything that could be eaten, worn or ridden.

Deep River Friends Meeting House near Jamestown. The earliest part was built in 1758. In 1875, it was torn down and replaced by a brick structure still in use. *Courtesy Friends Historical Collection, Guilford College, Greensboro, North Carolina.*

Their destination was Deep River, where they believed they would find a prosperous community and desperately needed supplies.

With the camp established at the meetinghouse and spreading along the road, one of the first orders given, on March 13, was, "A party of one officer and fifty privates from the Brigade of the Guards to parade immediately and march to Mendenhall's Mill. A guard will attend from headquarters."

Mendenhall's mill was very near the present bridge on Penny Road that crosses High Point City Lake. In 1781, George Mendenhall, who lived nearby with his wife, Judith Gardner Mendenhall, and their children, operated the mill. The mill was something over two miles south of Deep River Meeting.

The British remained there overnight, and a second order was issued by Cornwallis on the following day, March 14, saying, "The party at Mendenhall's Mill will be relieved at 12 o'clock this day—a sergeant and two of which relief will be sent immediately as an escort to the wagons to this mill where they will remain and be joined by the other part of the guard."

According to Mendenhall family tradition, after all the stored grain and foodstuffs had been commandeered, the soldiers drove off the only remaining milk cow. The lady of the house went to the officer in charge, stated her case and was allowed to lead the cow home.

On the morning of the fifteenth, all of the troops marched early toward New Garden Friends Meeting, where the first battle of that day took place, followed in the afternoon by the day's second (and major) battle, at Guilford Courthouse.

After his retirement, Newlin, a professor of history at Guilford College, teamed his knowledge of history with his knowledge of the local landscape, and wrote two accounts with plentiful local detail of lesser-known battles leading up to that at Guilford Courthouse. One, *The Battle of New Garden,* contains information used in this article. The second is *The Battle at Lindley's Mill.* Both are available from the North Carolina Friends Historical Society.

A Visit to "Old Jamestown" at the Annual Village Fair

The third Saturday in July is the day to explore "Old Jamestown" if you haven't already done it—or even if you have.

That is when the Historic Jamestown Society sponsors its annual Village Fair at the Richard Mendenhall Plantation at 601 West Main Street in Jamestown (across from High Point City Lake Park). The event is free (except for the hot dogs), and the hours are between ten and four o'clock. And there's plenty of shade under the big walnut trees.

All of the larger and most of the smaller buildings on the grounds of the plantation will be open. These include the 1811 Richard Mendenhall House, the old Pennsylvania-style bank barn, several outbuildings, the replica schoolhouse and also the Madison Lindsay Medical School.

They are supplied with furniture, pottery, household utensils, farming tools, textiles, medical instruments, spinning wheels, wagons and buggies, and all the other things we associate with rural life in the nineteenth century. The old meetinghouse in High Point City Lake Park will be open also, as this was once an important part of Old Jamestown. It sat at the end of Union Street, which once ran due south to cross Main (old Federal) and to run between Richard Mendenhall's house and his barn, past his tannery.

Jamestown was first settled about 1759. It became a chartered town in 1816, and most of these buildings represent those earliest years of its life.

Richard Mendenhall built the first portion of this house in 1811. It was on a lot in the village planned by his father, George Mendenhall, and named for George's father, James. Richard was a tanner and had a tan yard behind the house. *Courtesy Frederick P. Browning.*

Of unusual interest in the Mendenhall barn is the false-bottom wagon, one of only two known, which was used to transport slaves who were hidden under cargo and carried to the Midwest on the Underground Railroad. Though it isn't certain that the Quaker Mendenhall family was directly involved in this antislavery activity, they were actively engaged in the Manumission Society, and their sympathies were well known.

There are usually special performances. In 2003 and 2004, a local actress appeared as famous African American heroine Harriet Tubman. She was very engaging in her portrayal of this famous woman.

Each year there have been performances by a costumed group from the Outdoor Theater at Snow Camp, where the historical dramas *The Sword of Peace* and *Pathway to Freedom* are presented during the summer months. The performers usually appear in early afternoon.

Outside the Lindsay House is the medicinal herb garden, a project of the Cedarwood Garden Club. The garden now has brick walks, a millstone centerpiece and established plants that are identified with small signs.

Often attending is an archaeologist with his display of Native American spear points and similar items. Spinners and quilters will be at work demonstrating their practical skills in the Mendenhall House. There are games for kids, and some arts and crafts to work on: quilt fans, bonnets and cornhusk dolls. A blacksmith demonstrates what the old apprentice bonds used to refer to as the "art and mystery" of his craft.

There are likely to be other special events, such as the 2004 silent auction of an old claw-footed bathtub. This elderly beauty sat in regal splendor on a raised platform in a back second-floor room of the Richard Mendenhall House for many years, but the time came when it had to go to make room for something more historical—in this case, a restored loom.

This is an exceptional way for you and your family to spend some quality Saturday time.

Jamestown Friends Meeting House

The only job the small red brick building has now is to sit there and look interesting, and it performs that task very well. It faces one of the parking lots at High Point City Lake Park, and has a sign in front that says "Jamestown Friends Meeting House and Cemetery" and gives a brief history and description.

The building is about 190 years old. Approximately 25 years ago, it was restored by High Point under the supervision of the High Point Historical Society, which has overall responsibility for it. It was skillfully repaired, and the brick and stone foundation and chimney were returned to new condition. Since that time, it receives regular maintenance attention from the park staff. It is occasionally used for small weddings or meetings.

It survived because it was well built and because it probably never had the kind of heavy daily use that wears down even the best Carolina red brick. That does not mean that it was never a busy place, however.

The one-room structure was built by the George Mendenhall family—the original Jamestown developers—as part of their planned town, which they called Jamestown to honor George's father. Actually, the meetinghouse was just outside the original town limits, but it was situated prominently at the end of Union Street, which is now the street that enters the park.

Jamestown Quakers, who belonged to Deep River Friends Meeting, used it for midweek worship as early as 1818. Since the meetinghouse was on land retained by a family member, George C. Mendenhall inherited it and ownership then passed by his will in 1860 to the Commissioners of the Corporation of Jamestown.

Sometimes it was used as a school between about 1870 and about 1900, although there was a separate school building nearby for many years. When

The Jamestown Friends Meeting House, built about 1816. Beneath the trees in the background is a small old burial ground. *Courtesy of the author.*

Jamestown lost its charter, ownership of the meetinghouse reverted to the family, and eventually to Mary Mendenhall Hobbs, a great-granddaughter of George Mendenhall Sr. Mrs. Hobbs sold the building in 1915 to the Jamestown Primitive Baptist Church.

The congregation of the church was African American, and the building was used by this group until 1933, when the church's trustees sold the building to the City of High Point, which had already purchased much of the surrounding land for the waterworks dam and the park.

The Jamestown Primitive Baptist Church trustees named on the deed were Ezekiel Fuller and wife Mezeriah Fuller; Nat Martin and wife Bessie Martin; and David Hobson and wife Roda Hobson.

The Fullers lived very near the church, on Main Street in Jamestown. Minerva Mendenhall had given Mezeriah two lots in her 1900 will, and these lots were very near the present entrance to the park. The Fullers are shown on the 1900 census in Jamestown with two sons, William Fuller and Walter Fuller. Ezekiel's occupation is listed as "drayman," or driver of a freight wagon.

Mezeriah "Aunt Mez" Fuller was a trustee of the Primitive Baptist Church that bought the old meetinghouse in 1915. She lived nearby on a Main Street lot given to her by Minerva Mendenhall. *Courtesy Historic Jamestown Society.*

David "Hobson" is almost certainly David Hopkins, highly regarded employee of the Jamestown High School, the custodian and the manager of the school's Farm Life inventory of field acreage and livestock.

The small burial ground next to the meetinghouse contains few legible stones, but one of them is for Eliza Martin, wife of Nat, possibly the "Bessie" named as a trustee on the deed. She died in 1906, according to her broken stone.

This burial ground also contains graves that date from an earlier time. Both David Lindsay, who owned a general store and died in 1860, and his wife Sarah Dillon, who died in 1864, are buried there. Many graves have no stones at all, but in one instance, brand-new markers have replaced the old ones.

This is a time when it's difficult to find funding to maintain old buildings and burial grounds, so it's refreshing to know that—at least in this instance—someone is taking care of it.

Jamestown Quakers Walked the Walk

Among Richard Mendenhall's children, there were some who held fast to the Quaker beliefs, and who not only gave voice to antislavery sentiments, thus " talking the talk," but who also "walked the walk."

There remains in my mind more than a little doubt that fugitive slaves were hidden at the Richard Mendenhall Plantation, however. Many believe that they were. There is no real evidence either way.

It is known that Richard's younger brother, George C. Mendenhall, who lived in the old James Mendenhall House on Deep River, owned slaves that his first wife brought to the marriage. In later years, George C. and his second wife legally resettled some of those slave families in the Midwest and made plans to do so with the others. Those plans ended with the Civil War.

But what George C. was doing was in no way Underground Railroad activity. It was done cautiously, with careful attention to all details, but it was legal, open and aboveboard.

Richard Mendenhall died in 1851. Living in his house during the Civil War years were his widow, Mary, and two unmarried daughters, Minerva and Judith J., both teachers. Their brother, Nereus, was also a teacher and had been employed at New Garden Boarding School. All three were as devoted to education as they were to other Quaker tenets.

In 1865, at the end of the war, Nereus was working with the state authorities to reopen the state's public schools and to organize for the first time public schools for Negroes. His sister Judith volunteered to organize and teach such a school in Jamestown.

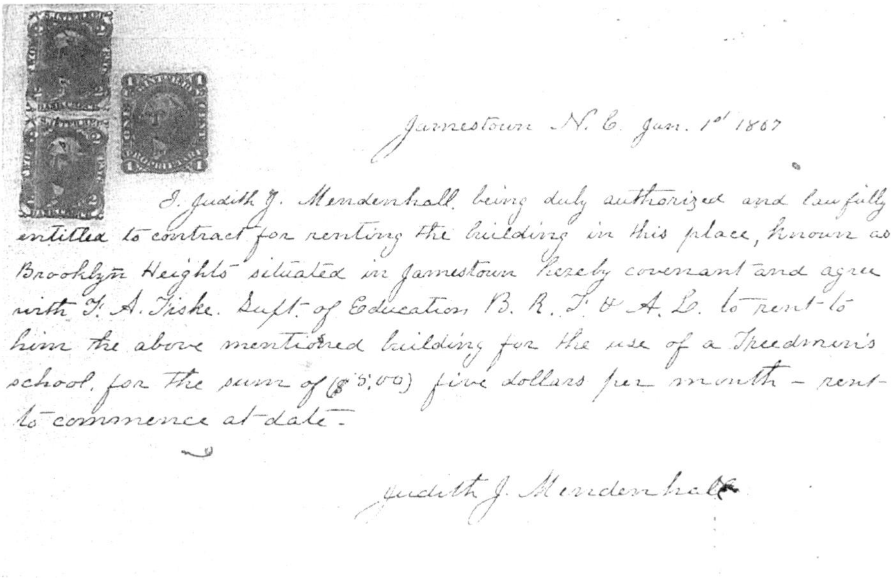

Jamestown N. C. Jan. 1st 1867

I. Judith J. Mendenhall being duly authorized and lawfully entitled to contract for renting the building in this place, known as Brooklyn Heights situated in Jamestown hereby covenant and agree with F. A. Fiske. Supt of Education B. R. F. & A. L. to rent to him the above mentioned building for the use of a Freedmen's school, for the sum of ($5.00) five dollars per month – rent to commence at date.

Judith J. Mendenhall

Judith J. Mendenhall wrote this contract to rent her building for a Freedmen School for five dollars per month. *Courtesy of the author.*

These schools were usually called Freedmen Schools, because they were operated under the authority of the Bureau of Refugees, Freedmen and Abandoned Lands, part of the new machinery operating state government, including public schools.

Perhaps no one will ever know for sure, but I've studied every scrap of information I can find that relates to the matter, and I feel confident that this school was held in the small brick schoolhouse that the Mendenhalls owned on old Union Street in what is now High Point City Lake Park. Union Street approximated the present entrance road to the park, and the school was somewhere along the west side of the road, probably about midway between Main Street and the brick meetinghouse.

A number of letters written by Judith to the bureau are on microfilm published by the National Archives. Her monthly reports are also reproduced.

Judith found that getting help was uphill work. She pleaded for funds to reimburse what she had spent on repairs to the building. Since she had not asked in advance, she did not get them.

In February 1868, she wrote to the quartermaster in Greensboro asking for rations: "If there is any way whereby assistance can be obtained I desire something for a few persons near me—Not at all for our own use, but to give to the starving. I do not know what is best. Of course 'They are a trifling set' but do they not necessarily require more care? If this is too great a trespass upon your time and patience, please to excuse me."

She did not keep the school going the next year, but informed authorities that the building would not be available, although it would be used by the freedmen for worship services and Sunday school.

Another Freedmen School was organized by Deep River Friends Meeting. After two years, it reported having two teachers and fifty scholars and was self-supported. Its final report in 1869 shows that the teacher was a person of color, but the name is not given, unfortunately.

A better-organized state education organization took over in 1870, with two departments, White and Negro. The Freedmen Schools, heavily supported by Quaker and like-minded organizations in Northern states, had done their best to bridge the chasm between slavery and freedom for five crucial years. It was a shaky start, but it was a start.

Minerva's Ghost Walks

Mary Jane Haney, an early president of the Historic Jamestown Society, says that a visitor to the Mendenhall Plantation who wanted to go into the old barn to look around sighted a costumed docent already heading that way, striding in her long skirt toward the closed double door. The visitor walked fast to catch up but then stopped short, because when the docent got to the door, she didn't reach out to the handle or take out a key, but just walked right through it.

At that moment (if there really was such a moment) the "ghost of Minerva" legend began, I believe, and it would end there, as well, if it depended upon additional sightings to keep it going. As far as I can determine, there have been no other sightings. There are creaking doors that close abruptly in the old house, which is to be expected in a nearly two-hundred-year-old house with many windows and doors and three chimneys. Volunteers who spend time there will likely shrug off these natural squeaks, slams and whooshes by saying, "There goes Minerva again."

In addition, there's a corner stairway that is pretty scary if there is no light on above it, especially so to a child standing at the bottom and looking up. An elderly local resident assures me that she remembered very well that she was afraid to go up those stairs when she visited the house as a child.

Why is all of this blamed on Minerva? And who was Minerva, anyway? That's a fair question, and here's a brief answer: She's the one who was there for so long.

Minerva Mendenhall was born in February 1813, the first child of Richard and Mary Pegg Mendenhall. She died in February 1900, and was buried in the Deep River Friends Meeting graveyard. As her father had put the date 1811 on the chimney of his house, we assume it was built by then, and Minerva was surely born there. She spent her entire life there, never marrying, and became the caretaker of all of her father's property as her siblings moved away. Papers in the Friends Historical Collection at Guilford College show that she was paying taxes on the several buildings that are now part of the Mendenhall Plantation, on several that are now in City Lake Park and on other properties that aren't so easy to identify.

Censuses show that she usually had several other people in her household. Sometimes we know from other sources that children lived with her, in one

Minerva Mendenhall, seated by her fireplace in the Richard Mendenhall House. She wears the traditional "inside" Quaker bonnet that would be covered by a larger bonnet when going out. *Courtesy Historic Jamestown Society.*

case a little girl unhappy with her father's second wife. Minerva may have taken boarders on occasion. There certainly was room for them. She usually had one or more hired helpers, whom she would have needed, especially as she grew older. She probably took in travelers who needed a place to spend the night.

She was a teacher. She apparently attended a female academy at Yanceyville to prepare for this career. When the state began to require certification of the teachers for its tax-supported common schools, she became certified and the skimpy records available show that she did teach in more than one district. She gave her occupation as "teacher" on at least one census. She is believed to have taught classes in her house, too—perhaps a primary subscription school.

In 1867, she was appointed Jamestown postmaster. Officially, the post office she ran was "20 rods from Deep River on the West Bank." I don't have a clear picture in my mind of how far 20 rods is, but I understand that Minerva had set up a special room on the side porch of the Mendenhall House to serve the purpose. She continued in that position until 1879, when Joseph S. Ragsdale was appointed. I'm pretty sure that the office itself would have been moved closer to the railroad depot at that time, but that's a guess.

None of the volunteers I contacted had any personal experience with a ghost at the Richard Mendenhall House, beyond the joking references to the tradition.

So that's the story on Minerva. Nowadays the ghost factor at Mendenhall Plantation is downplayed as being a flimsy and ephemeral topic, and a distraction from the serious business of interpreting history. It is. But it's hard to stop these things once they get started, and now the ghost has its own history.

This Old Book Is a Local Favorite

They Loved to Laugh, a novel written by Kathryn Worth and first published in 1942, caused a moderate stir locally because it was set principally in the Centre Friends Meeting area of southern Guilford and northern Randolph Counties in the 1830s, and—even more importantly—it had a chapter entitled "A Visit to Jamestown."

It went out of print after one reissue in 1956, after which it really dropped out of sight, disappeared from many library shelves and became something of a rarity. That is my excuse for never reading it until a friend loaned me a copy recently. This copy was a surprise, because it was a brand-new paperback from a 1996 reprint edition put out by Bethlehem Books, which specializes in literature for children and families. It is rated for grades eight and up.

The main character is a sixteen-year-old girl, Martitia, recently orphaned in a typhoid fever epidemic, who finds herself living in the Centre Friends Meeting neighborhood, in the home of a Quaker doctor and his family. The family includes a hardworking mother and daughter, as well as five sons who "loved to laugh," especially at someone else's expense, or so it seemed to Martitia. As an only child, she was quiet, shy and sheltered—a girl who had never been required to help with household duties.

Throughout, the author has used fictitious names, but familiar ones. Martitia, for instance, was quite a common girl's name here in the nineteenth century. Other familiar ones are used, such as Eunice, Barzellai, Clarkson, Addison and Abel. The surnames are equally evocative of the time and place: Gardner, Macy, Mendenhall, as well as the author's own name. Referring to her characters and story, Kathryn Worth states that her intent is to re-create the inward truth of historic character, not the outward accuracy of historic detail.

She did use two genuine names in her Jamestown chapter: George Mendenhall and Dr. Madison Lindsay. Other characters in the Jamestown chapter are subject to speculation. Perhaps she set down certain well-known physical and character traits, shook them up in a bag and assigned them higgledy-piggledy to her fictitious characters that had almost-familiar names. Prominent is Martitia's hostess, the paragon Sarah Gardner Mendenhall, who has a nose like George Washington's, but does everything extremely well, discusses current events with ease and cares for her aged father, Abel.

Near Jamestown, "over by Deep River," is the home of Madame de la Brousse, whom they visit in order to see her silk-weaving establishment. Since Martitia had learned to speak French from her mother, she is able to speak to Madame, who is delighted at the opportunity. The Frenchwoman is operating a silk factory of sorts, raising silkworms, spinning the silk and weaving silk cloth. This is an interesting section, describing in some detail a cottage industry that was very popular in this area of the Piedmont during the nineteenth century.

The book is packed with information on nineteenth-century households in rural North Carolina, where sheep were sheared, butter was churned, cloth was woven and nearly everything else that a rural family needed it found a way to produce on its own. In its handling of racial and gender issues, one is reminded in reading it that it was written for a 1942 audience, not for a current one.

So *They Loved to Laugh* is interesting history in several ways, and over the years has probably provided some fun for people named Macy, Mendenhall and Gardner, and for some Quakers of Centre and Deep River Meetings, in trying to work out Kathryn Worth's models for her characters.

Part II

Variety Added Spice

Not everyone was a Quaker settler. Newcomers and travelers of many stripes and shapes brought their own ideas and cultural baggage to this village.

Baptists Built an Early Meetinghouse

Not everyone was a Quaker in early Jamestown, in spite of the common perception of the little town. As soon as it was granted a charter by the North Carolina General Assembly in 1816, the village became a magnet for many whose future plans were not for farming, but were for trades that would benefit from a concentrated population. There were only two such places in Guilford County at that time—Greensboro, site of the courthouse, and Jamestown.

Among the earliest settlers, and also among those who later were attracted to the prospects offered here, there were quite a few Baptists. The denomination already had a substantial history in this area, dating from Shubal Stearns's arrival at Sandy Creek in the 1750s.

However, Jamestown's Baptists were members of the nearer congregation, which was at Abbott's Creek in present Davidson County. Attending worship services required a daylong trek, however. So in 1825, when local members were numerous enough to petition for dismissal from Abbott's Creek, they became an independent and regular church at Jamestown.

The old record book belonging to Abbott's Creek Primitive Baptist Church notes, in May 1825, "On the third Saturday in the present month at Jamestown a way was opened for Experience. Recd Elizabeth Poor." Soon afterward, "At a Meeting held at Jamestown on the fourth Saturday and Sunday following for June a way was opened for Receiving Experiences and Received into our fellowship Jeremiah poor Jesse field and wife by letter Alex Yates & wife."

Then, still in 1825, "A petition was handed in By Bro[r]. Beeson Requesting the Eldership of this church to meet those at Jamestown the second Saturday in this month to enquire into their qualifications in order to become a constituted body which petition was granted and appointed Elder Ashly Swaim Solomon Davis Alexander Thomas and Joseph Spurgin to attend to the same." This was apparently in July. In August, the final permission was given.

According to *History of the First Baptist Church 1825–1968*, published by First Baptist Church of High Point in 1969, the church was "constituted on September 3, 1825. It was called the Jamestown Baptist Church." In October of that year, Elder Ashley Swaim was called as pastor and continued to serve both at Jamestown and Abbott's Creek. In December, Isaac Beeson was chosen clerk. In January, Joseph Armfield and Jesse Field were elected deacons. There were about twenty-five members at this time.

When the congregation bought a lot for a church building, the trustees named for the "Missionary Society for Spreading the Gospel in the State of North Carolina" were Jesse Field, David Lindsay and Isaac Beeson. It was to be used by various groups of Christians for divine worship. The lot they purchased belonged to Nathan Mendenhall and was described in the deed as "being in the Western part of James Town in sd county containing half an acre of land known and distinguished by the eastern half of Number nine north-west agreeable to the Registered plan of said Town."

If you now go into the parking lot behind the buildings at 720 West Main Street, stand with your back to the old building in the middle—the old Reece-Harper Johnston-Bevan house—and look north, you are looking at the lot where the church was built. It stood until about 1875, according to *History of the First Baptist Church.*

In the years between 1829 and 1832, the Baptists of Jamestown became involved in "dissension and strife," as Baptists will do, and as Baptists were doing all around the country at that time. The disagreement was over—can you guess?—missions. Those interested in the details of the fallout from this turmoil can read a good account of it in the *History* referred to above, available in libraries.

In the case of Jamestown, the congregation that remained formed a mission church and became part of the Liberty Baptist Association when it organized in 1832. Messengers representing the church at that gathering were Elder William Burch, the pastor, Isaac Beeson and David Idol. The church remained with the Liberty Baptist Association during the following years, but it was never a large or very strong one. Its membership apparently averaged only twenty or so members.

The Sandy Creek Separate Baptist Church in Randolph County might have been the model for the Jamestown Baptists. Shubal Stearns organized the Sandy Creek congregation in 1755. *Courtesy North Carolina Office of Archives and History.*

In August 1850, the association held its annual meeting in Jamestown, according to Mary (Pegg) Mendenhall, who wrote of it in a letter to her daughter Minerva:

> *It is a great time among the baptists about here. they had their association in James Town this year—and altho it rained a great deal last night and the river was foaming with muddy water almost up to the Bridge Harris and his wife and some other woman I did not hear who was plunged this morning it is still raining and the folks are making their way to meeting to the two oclock Sermon.*

The letter is in the North Carolina Friends Historical Collection at Guilford College.

In 1859, after several church members had moved to the booming new town of High Point, those who attended a meeting in the church in Jamestown on July 23 voted unanimously and unceremoniously to transfer the Jamestown church there, and so ended the (first) Jamestown Baptist Church.

Some Methodist History Comes to Light

Facts about early Jamestown Methodists are pretty hard to pin down, at least for the time before 1878, when Oakdale Methodist was organized. A little later than that, in 1889, there was a Methodist church built about where the present Jamestown United Methodist now stands. It burned down in 1926, and was replaced the same year with a larger building.

But where was the Methodist Episcopal church that was borrowed in 1858 for "public preaching and religious exercises" by the Methodist Protestants who were holding their annual conference in Jamestown? The visiting Methodists were getting ready to open their Jamestown Female College near Scientific Street, and the minutes of their conference refer to this church. It was most likely in "old" Jamestown, near the college and the Masonic Hall, which was also used for some of the conference meetings.

A few new ideas arrived recently, courtesy of a generous correspondent who has been working on a biography of a nineteenth-century Methodist preacher named Reverend John E. Edwards, DD. In his later years, Edwards wrote some articles about his early days as a preacher, and these were published in a statewide Methodist publication generally referred to as the *Advocate*. It is in a couple of these that Edwards writes about Jamestown in 1833, as he recalled it in 1883. That is fifty years, you will note, so his recollections might not be perfectly accurate. This is part of what he wrote in the *Advocate* of June 13, 1883, about the village that was part of his "charge":

The Jamestown Methodist church was built in 1889. *Courtesy Historic Jamestown Society.*

> *I had ten or a dozen families, more or less; and, as well as I can recollect, one house used for public worship. I think it was a sort of school house, and served the purpose for religious worship for the denominations that chose to occupy it. It was a framed, wooden house, without ceiling or plastering, and I am not quite certain that it even had glass windows. My impression is that it had batten window shutters, and was partially fitted up with plain benches. It was a plain, primitive structure, without any enclosure around it, and wore an air of isolation, not to say of positive desolation. Jamestown was in the old Guilford circuit at the time of which I write.*

The recollection of a plain wooden building eliminates either the brick meetinghouse now in High Point City Lake Park, or the nearby brick school building that once was there. However, the building might have been the one built by the Baptists. Their deed stipulated that the piece of ground they purchased should be used for "all societies sects and denominations of Christians."

Edwards says that before his ordination, he preached his very first sermon in Jamestown, or "Jim Town." His mentor, Reverend Joshua Bethel, insisted one day that Edwards accompany him to Jamestown for a weekday meeting. About twenty people turned up:

> *Bro Bethel read the General Rules of the Societies, and then said, without any further consultation with me, that "Bro Edwards will now preach for you." I was seated on a bench outside of the pulpit, and did not respond to the announcement; whereupon he came down and took me by the hand and led me to the desk, and told me to preach. I was scared half out of my life. Fortunately for me, and without his knowledge, I had prepared a sort of a sermon—my first attempt in that line…I preached, or tried to preach. The delivery occupied 12½ minutes, as nearly as I could come at it. I wonder if there is anybody now living that heard my first sermon? What became of that house of worship?*

He writes also of a camp meeting held "in the woods bordering the village" in the fall of 1833. "There were several conversions, and an increase of members in the small society; and the next year, 1834, the village of Jamestown was connected with Greensboro as a sort of double station, and the Rev. Samuel S. Bryant was appointed to the charge."

With some luck, additional interesting Jamestown Methodist history might come this way.

Oakdale United Methodist Church evolved from a brush arbor to the present structure, and has always been part of the Oakdale Mill community. *Courtesy Frederick P. Browning.*

Jamestown Female College

In what was an ongoing competition with its parent denomination, the Methodist Episcopal Church, the North Carolina Conference of the Methodist Protestant Church worked up a plan for a female college, and in 1855 started looking for a good site. In 1856, when the annual conference was held at Moriah Church in Guilford County, George C. Mendenhall attended, carrying a petition signed by many Jamestown residents. He offered to give land for the school in Jamestown if the trustees would agree to the plan. To no one's surprise, they readily agreed. In 1858, at conference time, the session was held in Jamestown and construction of the school building was underway. The first session of the school started on July 14, 1859, and regular sessions were held until August 9, 1861, when fire destroyed the building.

The conference meetings were held in the Masonic Hall, home of Logan Lodge 121, Ancient York Masons. The name first proposed for the new school was Logan Female Seminary. This suggestion came from the committee headed by Calvin H. Wiley, who was at that time the state's superintendent

This monument on the campus of High Point University says, "Jamestown Female College. This marker contains brick from the Jamestown Female College opened by the Methodist Protestant church Jamestown N.C. 1859 and destroyed by fire 1861. Nikanthan and Thalean Literary Societies May 1, 1929." *Courtesy Frederick P. Browning.*

of public instruction, as well as an ordained minister. The name Logan didn't stick; perhaps it was just a gesture of thanks to the organization that provided the meeting space. However, "Logan" appeared a few years later as the earliest name put to Oakdale Cotton Mill.

Something that would be interesting to pursue would be the identities of the students. Fortunately, even though its life was very brief, it was a functioning institution during the 1860 census, so the surnames of the young women who were "pupils" in the "household" of its president, Jno. S. Ray, are given—all forty-seven of them. None of their first names appear, but their initials do. I see a little cluster of names, Branson, Hyslop and Young, that I'll bet come from upper Randolph County There's a Yancy from Virginia and a Fembleburk from South Carolina; all others are from North Carolina—a Coffin, a Kirkman, a Lamb, a Hobbs and so on. It's said that the young ladies finished off the 1861 school year after the fire at Beataville Academy in Davidson County.

The tract of land that belonged to the college was bounded by the south line of the old medical school lot on the northeast, by Scientific Street on the east, Kearns Avenue on the south, Robbins Avenue on the west and West Main Street on the north. In 1870, a Canadian family named Bertram purchased the land, kept it for about a year and then sold it and moved away.

My hunch is that they thought that they might find a warm welcome and good opportunities here, but that those did not materialize in the severely depressed post–Civil War atmosphere of Jamestown at that time.

The only physical remnants of the college to be found now are in a modest dozen or so bricks that form a base for a memorial monument on the campus of High Point University.

An 1849 Visit

In the late afternoon of a cold and snowy day in March 1849, two weary travelers arrived in the village of Jamestown in search of shelter.

One was Benson J. Lossing, and the other was his horse, Charley, both chilled to the bone and very tired. They had spent the day retracing the routes taken by British and Revolutionary armies leading to the famous 1781 encounter they had at Guilford Courthouse.

Lossing, a native of New York State, was a successful maker of woodcut engravings on his home ground, and was active in publishing. In 1849, he was beginning an exciting new project, touring Revolutionary battlefield sites, making sketches, interviewing residents and taking notes, all in preparation for what would become *The Pictorial Field-Book of the Revolution*, eventually published in 1859.

This day in 1849 had begun in Greensboro, where he had spent much of the night watching residents fighting a fire—without aid of fire engines, he noted—that consumed four buildings before a broad exterior chimney stopped it. All that excitement meant a late start the next day, but by ten o'clock Lossing had reached Martinville, the first stop on his itinerary. There he found that his contact, "Mr. Hotchkiss," was away from home, but the gentleman's daughter answered many of his questions. Was the "Hotchkiss" home he visited that of Mr. Hoskins? Anyway, Lossing sketched the battlefield and noted that his vantage point was the extreme western boundary of the field.

It had started snowing during the morning. At noon, with the snow still falling, Lossing left for the Quaker meetinghouse at New Garden. A wedding was in progress there. The groom was from Randolph County, Lossing said. This might help to date the visit, because there were only a handful of marriages at New Garden in the 1840s, and only one that could be found with a groom from Randolph. He was Frederick Henley and his bride was Sarah Jane Macy. The date was March 1, 1849.

Lossing also visited New Garden Boarding School nearby, whose superintendent at the time, Thomas Hunt, introduced him to his father, ninety-one-year-old Nathan Hunt. That worthy man shared some recollections of the time of the Revolution, when some of the dead and dying from local skirmishes and the Guilford Courthouse battle were brought to New Garden for care.

The afternoon wore on, the weather didn't improve and Lossing mounted Charley and headed them both toward Jamestown, over a countryside that he described as "very broken."

When he reached Jamestown, he found it to be "an old village situated upon the high southwestern bank of the Deep River." If this doesn't sound like the Jamestown you know, think of the height of the dam in High Point City Lake Park, and remember also that just downstream from the dam there is about a thirty-foot drop from the bridge on Main Street to the river below.

Since Lossing reported that most of the original Quaker inhabitants of Jamestown had come from Nantucket, we might infer that the lodging he found was in the George C. Mendenhall home on the West Fork riverbank, where the lady of the house at that time was Delphina Gardner Mendenhall, a descendant of Nantucket Quakers. Lossing also reported that the Jamestown inhabitants "do not own slaves, or employ slave labor, except when a servant is working to purchase his freedom," which is an interesting take on the actual situation. However, it does represent the views of the owner, whose first wife had inherited these slaves from her father. Mendenhall was obligated to care for them, but his goal was to train them for trades before setting them free, and he and Delphina did, in fact, take a number of them to lead free lives in the Midwest.

This lack of slave labor accounted for the "aspect of thrift" found in the local land and houses, Lossing thought, and gave the area a different appearance from that in the usual rural districts in the Carolinas.

When he left the next morning, three inches of snow had accumulated on the ground. Nevertheless, he was off for "the Yadkin" by way of Lexington and other points west.

Lossing's field book isn't great history, but it's fun to tag along with him in 1849 as he makes this trek through familiar territory, to see it as he saw it then. Even when he misunderstands what he sees and hears, he adds to our understanding of how it was.

Depression Years in Groometown

The author of *Where There's a Will, There's a Way* spent most of his youthful years in our neighboring community of Groometown, and attended Jamestown High School, where he graduated in the class of 1935. He writes about those years in his memoir, which was distributed only to members of his family and to a few select libraries. One copy is in the Jamestown Public Library, and there will probably be a long waiting list of people who will want to check it out.

It's a very readable book, written in an easy, unpretentious and straightforward style. There is some family background on Lasley's parents, Sallie Strader and Joseph Bernard Lasley, and some family pictures. By no means is it a genealogy, though. It is about Lasley, his parents, their other six children and a few close relatives and neighbors who made up his early world, spent first in the Cobbtown community of Rockingham County, then in Groometown and then for four years at North Carolina State University, where he received a mechanical engineering degree in the North Carolina State class of 1939.

Lasley's world in Groometown was on the land that his father purchased in the late 1920s. Lasley Sr. was ready to work hard to develop a tobacco farm that would provide a good living for his young family. The farm was on Freeman Mill Road (now Groometown Road). The neighbors were numerous Groome families to the north and the Venable, Ramsey, Osborn, Hennis and Kirkman families to the south.

The house wasn't much, but wasn't unusual for the times, either. It did have electricity—one bare bulb hanging from the ceiling in each room—but no electrical outlets and no plumbing. To make the kitchen a bit more than it was, Lasley Sr. built a long counter along one wall, put a sink in the center and ran a pipe outside for a drain. This at least saved carrying the dishpan to the back door to empty it. The stairway and upstairs rooms were unfinished. The home was poorly constructed and hardly worth the cost of repair, so the family lived with it, leaking roof and all.

The real effort went into the essential matter of establishing the farm. First a stable was built, then a horse bought and then a combined garage and pack house constructed with a cellar underneath. The purchase of a cow came next, followed by fences to keep her in. A hen house and log barns for tobacco completed the list of buildings. And, of course, tobacco was planted.

This book gives a remarkably full and detailed account of family life, mostly ordinary events, and a few very unusual ones. Those of us who remember those years realize that nearly everyone we knew was poor by today's standards. "Use it up, Wear it out, Make it do, Or do without" were words to live by. No one was ashamed of it; it's just the way it was.

When something really important was needed, "Where there's a will, there's a way" was Lasley's mother's attitude, and thus the name of his book. It's the attitude that found a way for Lasley to attend North Carolina State.

The author, James B. Lasley, who now lives in Charlotte, says that when his brother and two of his sisters urged him to write his recollections, he decided to give it a try, and he just began to jot down stories as they occurred to him. The more he wrote, the more he remembered, and he kept at it for three years before deciding that was enough. A cousin served as editor. Between the two of them, they did a bang-up job. What a generous gift he made to the intended recipients, the sixty-two direct descendants of Sallie and Joseph B. Lasley.

Part III

These Places Still Stand

Still here, in spite of it all, are interesting old places with stories to tell. The town's most visible building—called by both its old name, the Jamestown School, and its current one, the Jamestown Public Library—was saved largely through the efforts of former students, and it remains a vital part of the community. Other old structures were saved by individuals, families, organized groups or disorganized benign neglect.

Will the Potter House Be Restored?

The picturesque old Isaac Potter House at 211 West Main Street in Jamestown caught fire on the night of January 5, 2002. Now, the word is that it will be restored.

This assurance comes from the owner, who says that the log and frame building will be restored to "just like it was."

Reports of the fire at the time said that it probably looked worse than it was, and that it destroyed the roof but not the logs. The wood-burning stove being used by a Jamestown resident who was living in the house at the time probably caused the fire. A preservation consultant from the state's cultural resources department has examined the house and found it suitable for restoration. That is very good news, because it is an important element in Jamestown's National Register Historic District.

No one knows exactly when the original log part of the house was built, but the date of about 1819 is usually given. That is when Isaac Potter bought his land. An architectural survey that was done in 1979 says that additions were made about 1890. The enormous chimney at the western end is its most prominent feature. Was it always that big or was it enlarged later? Old-timers don't agree. Anyone who has spent a cold winter day in the house will agree that the big old fireplace creates a mighty draft, though.

Potter family tradition says that the original log building was used as a store between about 1819 and 1826, and then as a residence. Isaac was a farmer, according to censuses, but two of his sons, Isaac Potter and Henry Potter, had brief careers as millers just before the Civil War. One of the last of the

The Potter House before the fire. The original log building dates from no later than 1819. It has been used as a store, school, residence and the 1976 bicentennial headquarters. *Courtesy Historic Jamestown Society.*

Potters to live in the house was "Aunt Mary" Potter, fondly remembered as a teacher who kept a small subscription school in her home for an unknown period of time. She died in 1913.

The quaint old place was one of many Jamestown properties that William G. Ragsdale Jr. purchased in the 1950s to save from neglect or demolition. Various tenants have lived there since then.

In 1974, Mrs. Ragsdale made it available to the Guilford County American Revolution Bicentennial Commission to use as its headquarters. The commission's coordinator and the executive secretary kept business hours in the old building for the better part of three years as the organization did its work. The coordinator enjoyed working in the house, she says, and remembers that it was pretty comfortable most of the time, although there were a few shivery winter days. The location was ideal for the headquarters, being central to High Point, Greensboro and Winston-Salem.

Now, in 2005, it seems to be waiting patiently, anchored firmly by its huge chimney so far, but in danger of being uprooted by encroaching vegetation.

Potter Farm Is the Keystone to Jamestown's Historic District

The Potter House still awaits restoration.

Why is it important that this beat-up old house presently moldering away under a tarp, its condition steadily deteriorating, be restored and preserved? Why do people care?

The house itself began as a basic log structure of V-notched logs built on a stone foundation. It was probably built about 1819, which is when Isaac Potter bought the land that it stands on from David Beard. Actually, Potter was in possession as early as 1815, or so says a tax list of that date, so the log portion of the house could date from that time, or even earlier. The frame addition was built about 1890, according to a family member. The massive stone chimney on the west end dominates the whole visually.

Potter's purchase of land from David Beard was only the first in a series. He bought land adjoining it from James Talbot in 1819, and more from Jesse Field in 1825. These three tracts gave him about 280 acres. One corner of the original tract was in the middle of Deep River, but the land was all on the east side of the river, both north and south of the fork. Solomon Haworth was south of Potter; Richard Mendenhall was west and on the other side of the river; and Jesse Field still had some land north of the Salisbury Stage Road, on the other side of the road from Potter's house, until Potter bought that land, too, in 1838. At that time, the road was called the Greensboro Road, and we still call it the Greensboro–High Point Road (or Main Street).

What Potter had, in today's terms, was the land in the Deep River loop down as far as the railroad bridge; the land north of the railroad as far east as Dillon Road and a bit beyond, I think; and all of the land that Forestdale, the school, the shopping center and the businesses on the west side of Main Street rest upon. How far north it went, I don't know, but I think to Perry Road.

The Potter Farm, for that's what it was, was the connector for Old Jamestown west of the river and New Jamestown east of the river, the keystone that both rested against and tied them together.

Between 1819 and 1826, the log building was used as a store. The Potter family used it as a residence after that time. It was small, but all (or almost all) log cabins were small and that never seemed to stop families from growing within their walls. Why Isaac moved his family at that time isn't certain, and where it had lived previously isn't certain, either.

Isaac was born in Somerset County, Maryland, about 1787, a son of Henry and Sarah Potter, who moved the family south in stages, stopping temporarily in Pittsylvania County, Virginia, before coming along to Guilford County by 1804. The known children of Henry were Isaac and Mary. There was probably also a daughter, Nancy; a young woman of that name married James Talbot in 1815, perhaps the James who sold land to Isaac. Another child of Henry was probably Solomon, who married Martha Ferguson. Likely there were others we do not know about. Mary apparently never married, and she is buried at Deep River Friends Meeting cemetery.

Henry died in 1816. Isaac by that time had married Nancy Gossett, and she died in 1822, but she and Isaac had four children by then: Abraham, Minerva, Eliza and Isaac Jr. Isaac Sr. married again, in 1827, this time to Lois Kersey, and the couple had three children: Henry, Mary D. and Corinna. Lois was a Quaker, and some of the descendants were as well.

Abraham moved to Missouri and died there by 1840. Minerva married and soon moved to Kansas. Eliza married Henry M. Briggs, a coach maker in later years, and they remained in the vicinity. Mary D. and Corinna remained at home, unmarried.

The half brothers, Isaac Jr. and Henry, teamed up to go into the milling business in 1857, purchasing an old mill site on Bull Run that had been used for various purposes over many years, the turnover of owners indicating that none had been very profitable. In 1861, Cyrus P. Mendenhall purchased the site for a cotton mill, used it instead for a gun factory during the Civil War and then as a cotton factory. Oakdale Cotton Mill is there now.

Isaac Sr. died in 1864. Isaac Jr. moved at some time during the next decade to Minnesota with his wife Mary (Hunt) and their children. Henry became the agent at the railroad depot in Jamestown, and lived in the old log house with his widowed mother Lois and unmarried sisters Mary and Corinna, both of whom died by 1913.

In 1873, Henry married widow Lonora Reynolds Haworth, who died ten years later. They had four children: Lois Gertrude, Mary Edna, Robert Erle and Bertha Reynolds. Bertha died as an infant, but the three older children were known and remembered until recent times.

The eldest, Lois Gertrude, married and later moved to Buffalo, New York. The sisters raised Bob, only four when his mother died. As a young man, he worked as a shoemaker, moved west, married, divorced and finally went to Buffalo, where he lived with his widowed sister, Lois Gertrude Lambert. After his death, however, he came home and was buried at Deep River Friends in 1949.

It was Mary Edna, usually called Edna (she signed her name M. Edna), who lived in the little house. It was probably she who doubled the size of it by

Henry Potter (1829–1895), who, with brother Isaac Jr., purchased an old mill site on Bull Run where Oakdale Cotton Mill was later established. Henry was afterward the railroad agent at Jamestown Depot. *Courtesy Historic Jamestown Society.*

adding the frame addition to its west side in about 1890. She was a teacher, and is very well remembered for keeping a small subscription school in the house. Perhaps that's why she built the addition. She's also remembered for selling land, bit by bit, to neighbors who built homes along Main Street, and to the school for its Farm Life School farm, and later for the brick school building that still stands. She died in 1970.

Isaac Potter's land was not divided among his heirs until 1896. The records of that division show where the heirs were, as well as exactly what land members of the family owned.

The Historic Jamestown Society was given a number of small artifacts from the Potter family—a Quaker bonnet that belonged to Mary Haworth Reynolds, who was Henry Potter's mother-in-law; the 1819 deed in which Isaac Potter purchased land from David Beard; Gertrude Potter's autograph album; a folding umbrella; and other items. A photo of Bob Potter was among them.

The thing about very old buildings such as the Potter House is that we begin to realize that they don't belong to whoever holds the paper at the

The Potters and their friends about 1895. *Front row, left to right*: Bob Potter, Edna Potter, Marie Reuche and Bascom Bundy. *Back row*: Annie Johnson Bundy, Gertrude Potter, Claud Lamb and Dora Bundy. *Courtesy Historic Jamestown Society.*

moment. We get possessive; we think they belong to all of us. We want to count on their being right there.

A town that prides itself on its historic past, and that would like to use that past to attract visitors, should take care to preserve its significant historical treasures at all costs.

Gardner-Wiley House

Sandra "Sandy" Wiley Overly, the oldest daughter of Samuel Richardson Wiley and his wife, Estelle McCormack, now lives in the old Gardner-Wiley House, appreciating its elegant Federal detail as well as its family associations. The house, at 5003 Grandover Parkway, sits well back from the street, dignified and unpretentious among its flashier neighbors. It has a very nice new front porch, though that word doesn't quite do justice to the expanse of floor and columns and roof as wide as the house.

Sandy remembers growing up on this place, when it was tough to keep the dairy farm going through the lean years. She also recalls that her father later won wide recognition for his corn crops and advanced farming methods.

But, when the interstate was built, the farm was cut in half and its life as a dairy farm ended. The cows could not cross the road, and farm machinery wasn't allowed on the interstate.

Stephen Gardner, a Nantucket Quaker who settled in Guilford County in 1772, built the old house on a large tract of land in 1827, three years before his death. The two-story brick house has a central hallway, but otherwise conforms to the "Quaker plan." Gardner's youngest son Abel inherited it, and he and his wife Abigail Pinkham lived in the house until 1856, when they joined other abolitionists who were leaving the South for the Midwest.

Abel Gardner sold the house and a large tract of land, which included a gold mine, to Shannon Wiley, who was purchasing it for his son William Millis Wiley, a teacher, merchant, postmaster and legislator. The latter was supposed to provide a home for his two unmarried sisters, and he did, but they both later married. So did William, to Julia Idol. From William the property passed to his son William Gaston Wiley, a machinist and dairy farmer, and from him it went to Samuel Richardson Wiley, Sandy's father.

Following Sam's death in 1983, Sandy and her husband, John Louis Overly Jr., and their daughter Jane took up residence. By then, the neighborhood along Wiley Davis Road had changed dramatically, with the addition of the Wiley Park development and Trailwood.

The Gardner-Wiley House was built in 1827 by Nantucket Quaker Stephen Gardner. His son Abel sold it in 1856 to Shannon Wiley, whose descendants have lived there ever since. The early deeds included the Gardner Hill Mine, later sold separately. *Courtesy Sandra Wiley Overly.*

There had been rumors of even greater changes to come when Anheuser-Busch announced it had options to buy more than a thousand acres between Groometown Road and Vickrey Chapel Road. There would be a brewery, it was said. No, it would be a theme park. Neither of these panned out, but developer Joseph Koury, who had purchased those options, revealed his plan for Grandover in 1993.

Well, there it is, a done deal, and let that be a lesson to us all. As you wait for a light so you can turn where once you drove straight through, you might brood about the big old metaphorical steamroller that passed through this neighborhood not so long ago.

Not quite everything got flattened, though. There's still a pleasant bit of old Wiley Park left, and, even better, a bit of the time before Wiley Park, when it was a farm run by the Wiley family.

Sam Wiley had the perspicacity to get his house put on the National Register of Historic Places in 1975, and to preserve twenty-three acres of land, along with some of the old outbuildings.

It's a beauty, and, "Well, it's our home," says Sandy.

Three Signs Down and Quite a Few More to Go

Have you noticed the latest Jamestown Historical Marker, at 603 West Main Street? It makes three down (well, up) and, uh, quite a few to go. This one is "Home of Richard Mendenhall c. 1811." If the town council and others have their way, it will be just one of many that will help guide a walking tour around the town, and will be Jamestown's unique contribution to the Bicentennial Greenway.

The now-familiar dark brown cast-metal signs with the colorful Jamestown seal medallion in a curve at the top and gold-colored lettering are in the style established by a resolution of the Town of Jamestown in November 2002.

Getting a firm line on exactly when and where the inspiration for this project began is probably impossible. However, Jamestown's town clerk, Martha Wolfe, provided the date when the first one was ordered, September 2002, when it was ordered for Steve Crihfield on behalf of the Old Jamestown School Association. That one, the "Jamestown Public School" historical marker, was probably set in place in November of that year.

By that time, councilmen Keith Volz, Steve Crihfield, Martha Wolfe and Vic Gilliland had been named to a special historical signs committee, and a resolution had been passed setting standards for the markers and suggesting sites for additional ones.

The first of Jamestown's distinctive brown signs went up to commemorate the Jamestown Public School. *Courtesy Frederick P. Browning.*

"Oakdale United Methodist Church," the second marker, went up in front of the church on Oakdale Road in 2004 at about the time that the church and parsonage were nominated for the National Register of Historic Places.

Jamestown now has four different kinds of historical signs. The oldest variety, represented in town by only one specimen, is the official North Carolina highway historical marker at the western town line. It directs the attention of the passerby to "Beard's Hat Shop," once located one and one-third miles north on Penny Road. It is sign no. J13 of this statewide series, which makes it an early one in the J group that now goes up to 88. For instance, the Greensboro "Sit-Ins" sign is J79. The J series covers Rockingham, Guilford, Stokes and Forsyth Counties.

Next oldest in town is the pair of white wooden "Jamestown Historic District" signs marking each end of the National Register Historic District that was created some years ago. One marker is near the second Coffin House, and the other is on the north side of Main Street, west of 720 West Main. The Historic Jamestown Society maintains them, which is uphill work sometimes.

Then there are several signs erected by the Colonel John Sloan Camp #1290, Sons of Confederate Veterans. These are black-bordered, black-

The Reece House, also called the Harper Johnston-Bevins House, has porches on both sides because Main Street was moved to curve around its front in the 1920s. *Courtesy Frederick P. Browning.*

printed, silver-colored cast-metal signs resembling the North Carolina highway historical ones. "Mendenhall, Jones & Gardner Confederate Gun Factory" is on Oakdale Road near Harvey Road, and identifies that outfit as Oakdale Cotton Mill's predecessor at its present location. The "H.C. Lamb Confederate Gun Factory" sign on Guilford College Road near the power lines has been taken down for road construction—temporarily, we hope. Both of those signs were put up in 1988. The following year the "North Carolina Armory at Florence" sign was placed on East Fork Road near its Penny Road end. The Jamestown Rifles plaque the organization installed at Gibson Park could be included here, but it deserves more attention, and will get another column at another time.

At the time the resolution was passed by the town and the committee was formed, the following were suggested as possible sites for additional signs: both Coffin houses, Madison Lindsay, Potter House, Magnolia Farm, Mendenhall Store, Quaker Meeting House, Oakdale school, community well, mill and mill village, Jamestown Depot and Old Jamestown (City Lake). There are several other interesting sites as well—Holton mill, Harper Johnson and site of the Freedmen's School, among them. My personal first choice would be at the south end of the Penny Road bridge over High Point City Lake, the original site of the first Mendenhall Mill and House (circa 1763).

The signs aren't cheap, about $1,500 to $2,000, apparently, probably depending on how lengthy the text is. The property owners are expected to pay for them, and first apply to the town for approval. But the town orders them and then puts them solidly in place.

Lindsay Medical Building

The early plat of Jamestown that was recorded with the county register of deeds about 1812 shows the name "Scientic" on a street now known as "Scientific." Many of us can remember driving north on that street from Kivett Drive and then, at the Main Street stop sign (before there was a light), slowly inching out, peering to the left around the sloping rise of ground that hid oncoming traffic. If it was clear, there was a quick look to the right and another to the left before making a mad dash out.

On top of that inconvenient little hill to the left was a dilapidated wooden house that has a very long history. The structure was cut in half and hauled away in 1983, the low hill was leveled and an office complex was built on that corner. The old building was carried slowly and carefully on a big flatbed a short distance east to a spot at the end of the Mendenhall Plantation parking lot, where it came to rest under the care of the Historic Jamestown Society.

Location really *is* important, so the house seems diminished now without its prominent elevation and corner spot. However, it is there and it is upright. Its two halves are reattached. It is whole, safe, painted and heated. It performs several useful functions, too. It provides a good meeting room, for one thing. For another, it now has a furnished nineteenth century–style physician's office, which represents one of the building's historical functions. It demonstrates a long continuum of Jamestown's history. And it's a really interesting example of early-nineteenth-century architecture and construction practices.

Experts have made estimates on when it was built, some saying as early as 1800, and others being more cautious and guessing no later than 1820. Studies conducted in 1997 say that the house is made up of two buildings spliced together. The earliest part contains the larger rooms at the back. Attached to it was another building of two stories, with four smaller rooms. This study suggests that one or both buildings may have been moved to the Scientific Street site. Both sections were built of horizontal wooden boards.

The lot it was standing upon was purchased by 1813 by "Jno. Charles." He was probably the John Charles who was the first Jamestown postmaster, appointed in 1811. So, it's possible that the lot—perhaps the house—was the site of Jamestown's first post office. In 1819, the lot was sold to David Lindsay, who had set up his storehouse cater-corner to it on land purchased in 1816 from another member of the Charles family.

The year 1819 is the date when a former boarder at the Lindsay home, a young man named Marmaduke T. Mendenhall, who had been reading Latin with his kinsman George C. Mendenhall, left Jamestown to read medicine with a Dr. Watson in Greensboro. He then went to Philadelphia to attend medical lectures for a year. He returned to Jamestown in 1823, and was probably the first doctor in the village. Here we have another probably-possibly-maybe situation: perhaps he set up his office in that corner house. After he married in 1825, he moved to South Carolina.

The new doctor in town was Dr. Isaac James Madison Lindsay, a nephew of David Lindsay. Madison, as he was usually called, was just twenty-one in 1825, a doctor who was probably very new to his profession. Since he took students to read medicine under his care, he earned local fame as the director of a "medical college." The phrase calls to mind something grander than this establishment actually was, but in those early days it may have been appropriate. It was short-lived, anyway. Dr. Lindsay moved his practice to Greensboro about 1830. Part of the legacy of the school was the presence of rumors about graves being robbed in the nearby churchyard to provide cadavers for study.

Four of his students are known to have become doctors: Shubal G. Coffin, John Milton Worth, Joseph A. Weatherly and George D. Mendenhall. Two of these, Coffin and Worth, later attended medical lectures at the new Transylvania University Medical Department in Lexington, Kentucky, so their training under Dr. Lindsay was not considered complete, apparently. Another student, Dr. George D. Mendenhall, set up a medical practice in the same building by 1838, and sometime after 1840 moved to Virginia. That may have ended the old building's use as a doctor's office, because Dr. Shubal Coffin was the next town doctor, and he lived and practiced medicine in his home, which was a short distance east.

David Lindsay sold the old corner property to Alexander Robbins of Randolph County in 1857. Robbins's daughter, Martha Robbins Tilden, who was born in the old house, said that her father had come to town to be the secretary and treasurer of the building committee of Jamestown Female College, which began construction about 1858 just off Scientific Street, south and west of the house. Many of Dr. Lindsay's old medical books remained in the house, she said, and she recalled looking at them as a child.

The Madison Lindsay House. In the 1820s, this building housed the medical practice of Dr. Isaac James Madison Lindsay and the students who read medicine under his guidance, and stood at the corner of Main and Scientific Streets. Now, in its new home, it adjoins the Mendenhall Plantation parking lot. *Courtesy of the author.*

In 2001, James Mills, a Thomasville police officer with a special interest in medical history and artifacts, helped the Historic Jamestown Society to develop materials for a nineteenth-century physician's office replica.

Among the many tenants of the old house prior to 1983 were Mary and Rhodema Horney, who were private nurses, and lived there during the 1920s, earning a good reputation for their care of new mothers and babies.

The late Martha Tilden Hay was a descendant of the Robbins family who took a special interest in the study and restoration of the building after it was moved. She was instrumental in having it taken on as a project by a University of North Carolina–Greensboro Architectural Conservation class headed by Professor Jo R. Leimenstoll. Students examined everything in the old place, counting the number of paint and wallpaper layers and noting their colors, patterns and styles. They took note of locations of old "ghost marks" that show former partitions and chair rail traces. They produced measured drawings of floors, ceilings, walls, windows and doors. The very interesting results of their work are packed into a thick binder. Many of the old wallpapered areas have been left "as is" so that visitors can see the patterns. There are also areas where the old construction details can be viewed.

Walls can talk, after all, and can tell some good stories, too.

Second Coffin House

The fourth in the new series of Jamestown's historical signs is now in place, purchased by the Historic Jamestown Society and set up securely by the town's public works department. It identifies the second home owned by Dr. Shubal G. Coffin at 109 West Main Street.

Since being built by Coffin about 1855, it has had many other occupants, some residential and currently commercial.

Through thick and thin, good times and bad, Jamestown probably has always had at least one doctor living and practicing in the community, at least since about 1819. There were times when one had to be sought out

The second Coffin House. Dr. Shubal Gardner Coffin built this house in the 1850s to be near the North Carolina Railroad. *Courtesy Frederick P. Browning.*

and recruited. That may have been true in the case of Shubal Gardner Coffin, because he was practicing in Wadesboro in Anson County before he moved back here and set up an office in his home, now known as the Coffin-Robbins-Tilden House, on Main Street

However, he was well known in Jamestown, having grown up near Deep River Meeting House on the farm owned by his parents, Abel and Rhoda Gardner Coffin. A hand-drawn map in the files of Deep River Friends Meeting shows the Abel Coffin place east of the meetinghouse, on the south side of what was old Red Road, now more or less followed by Wendover. Shubal's mother, Rhoda Gardner, was the daughter of Stephen Gardner, who built the fine brick house in 1827 that still stands off Grandover Avenue south of Jamestown. So, Shubal's background was Nantucket Quaker on both sides, and Shubal himself was a member of Deep River Friends.

Shubal was born in 1809. When young Dr. Madison Lindsay set up his medical practice in Jamestown at the southwest corner of Federal (Main) and Scientific, Shubal Coffin became one of the students who read medicine with him. This would have been in the 1827–29 period. Other known students of Dr. Lindsay were Milton Worth and George D. Mendenhall. All three of these men later practiced medicine, Dr. Milton Worth in Randolph County and Dr. George D. Mendenhall in Grayson County, Virginia.

The medical school came to an end about 1829 or 1830, when Dr. Lindsay established a practice in Greensboro. At about the same time, Shubal was "complained of" by Deep River Friends for attending a marriage accomplished contrary to discipline; attending a place of diversion and taking part in it; and deviating from plainness in dress. Coffin refused to recant and was disowned. In 1831, he and Milton Worth entered Transylvania University's Medical Department as students for a one-year medical course.

In 1836, in Wadesboro, he married Laura Mendenhall. She was the daughter of Dr. William Mendenhall, who grew up in Jamestown in the old Mendenhall House on Deep River, one of the children of George Mendenhall. William owned the lot on which the Coffin-Robbins-Tilden House now stands. William had studied medicine with Dr. David Caldwell in the famous "Log College," and moved to Anson County, where he spent the rest of his life.

Shubal and Laura were living in Jamestown by 1840. I think perhaps Laura's father gave them the lot where they built the house in which they lived and raised a family. Among their children was William Edwin, born in 1849, who became a railroad official, and whose daughter Lucy married William G. Ragsdale Sr. Jamestown's Lucy C. Ragsdale High School is named for her.

In 1846, Shubal returned to Transylvania University to receive an honorary MD degree. He was active in community affairs, serving on boards and committees, often witnessing legal papers and buying and selling land and mineral rights. He was among those who watched with great interest as plans for a railroad were put forth in the 1850s, and, if tradition is true, actively sought to influence exactly what path the rails would follow through Jamestown. He favored the idea of laying them right along Federal (Main) Street so that it would be most convenient to his home and office. When it became clear that the line would run south of the village, he moved.

He chose a site near the tracks, and aligned his new board and batten house with its handsome extra-large windows so that he could easily sit on his front porch and see the depot and watch trains coming in from Greensboro. There's no certain date on the house, but "about 1855" is the guess usually stated.

In his later years, he lived in High Point, and he died in 1881.

Davis House

She was born in the house at 209 West Main Street in Jamestown in 1921. Now, as an energetic and attractive octogenarian, Jean Davis Harrison sits in her comfortable home off Westchester Drive in High Point and explains why she only lived in the house until 1930, and why the house is now usually referred to as the Frazier House rather than the Davis House.

Since its 1985 rezoning, the solid and dignified old home at 209 West Main Street has housed several commercial operations. The latest one is Magnolia Day Spa (which boasted beautiful and memorable decorations at Christmastime) and, before that, the *Jamestown News*.

This neighborhood—which includes the Jamestown Public Library in the old 1915 school building, the large 1950s Forestdale development and the houses on the south side of Main Street (in fact everything from the river east to Ragsdale Road)—was the old Potter farm. Since Isaac Potter began buying land in 1819, his descendants that lived in the old Potter House (the one that still doesn't have a new roof and is now almost hidden from view) owned most or all of it.

It was from Mary Edna Potter, her friend and neighbor, that Jean's mother, Laura Ham Davis, purchased a 2.03-acre tract in 1915. The lot ran from the macadam road (Main Street) south to the Southern Railway right of way. Laura Davis's husband, Venner Eugene Davis, built the house on it in 1916. He was a carpenter and he did much of the work himself, although at the

The Jamestown Public Library. The Jamestown Public School was built in 1915 as a county public boarding high school serving the western part of Guilford County. In early years, it had two dormitories. It was opened as a public library in 1988. *Courtesy Frederick P. Browning.*

same time he was working at the Johnson Shoe Manufacturing Company located on Oakdale Road.

Laura and Venner Davis had four children when they moved into their fine new house, and two more children were born there, Mary Louise in 1919 and Jean in 1921. Older daughter Grace was married in the front parlor of the house in 1924 and her daughter, Nancy Mildred Payne, was born there in 1926. Mary Louise's funeral was held in the house in 1929, and in that same year there was another funeral, that of J. Marvin Anthony, husband of the Davis's daughter Mildred.

More painful memories for the family were coming, though, for 1929 was the year the Depression began, and it hit the family hard. Mortgages taken out to help finance construction of the house could not be paid, and Laura and Venner lost the home they had built. The Davis family, along with many other good people, had an extremely rough going during the next few years. Jean remembers it as a time when her parents struggled to keep a roof overhead and food on the table. Her father was hired for a WPA job as a garden supervisor, and her mother worked as a live-in caregiver for Dr. and Mrs. Gordon, who both were elderly semi-invalids at that time.

The new owner of the Davis house in 1933 was Lottie R. Nelson, and she and husband Robert A. Baker sold the property to C.E. and Nettie N. Frazier in 1945. It is the Frazier name most people now have attached to the house because the Frazier family lived there for so long—about forty years. They were good stewards. The property has always looked cared-for and substantial.

A Davis descendant, Susan Bullock of Reidsville, has documented the history of the Davis House, as well as of the Ham and Davis families, and very kindly provided written records from her extensive research, as well as photos of the house. I'm grateful to her, to Jean Davis Harrison and to Jim and Janet Blackburn of Jamestown, who engineered our meeting.

Old Store House

You may have noticed that the old brick building at the entrance to City Lake Park has been spruced up. Amazing what a little routine maintenance can do for the elderly. With a new roof and some fresh paint on the trim, it looks pretty good for a structure that passed its century mark a long time ago.

Richard Mendenhall built the squarish two-story brick building in 1824. Cornerstones at the top corners of the west wall show "R.M.M." (the only known evidence that the builder had a middle name) on one, and "1824" on the other.

The High Point Museum is responsible for High Point's historical assets, such as this building and the old meetinghouse in the park, but there is never enough time and money to do it all. Even the important old relics have to get in line and wait their turns for repairs and general upkeep.

There are many questions that might be asked of the structure. What's with that funny little shallow outside hearth on the east side of the building, the one with the massive paving stones set in front of it? Were there ever steps up to that second-story door on the back of the building? The answer is surely yes, but what did they look like? Was there ever a block and tackle arrangement over the door to help lift and lower heavy loads? There's no sign of one now.

Why is there no doorway between the two cellars? Why is there no way to get into either one through the building itself? Each one has a bulkhead entrance on the street side of the building.

It is generally assumed that the building was intended for commercial use, rather than residential. Most believe that Richard Mendenhall used it in his tanning business. His house was across the street, and his tan yard was behind his house, downhill. But the Store House would have been a useful space to work on the prepared hides and to store the various grades that he produced. He probably made basic leather goods such as harnesses

The Richard Mendenhall Store House was photographed about 1934 when High Point City Lake Park was being developed. A sign at the left by the old dirt road announces that the park is closed. The photographer was L.R. Winslow. *Courtesy Library of Congress, Prints and Photographs Division, Historic American Buildings Survey, Reproduction Number HABS, NC, 41-JAMTO, 3-1.*

and belts. He wrote a treatise on his trade, "A Sketch on Tanning," that was published in the *Southern Friend* (volume twenty-eight, number one, 2006).

Old family business account records kept at the Friends Historical Collection at Guilford College also indicate that a general stock of household items and foodstuffs was also on sale.

There are four large rooms in the building, two down and two up. They have very high ceilings. The windows are large, so the interior lighting is quite good, and there is a pleasant, open feeling in the large rooms. At some point in the past, a bathroom upstairs and a kitchen downstairs were partitioned off in the northeast corner. The only plumbing in the building is there.

This is a genuine brick building, so the walls are the thickness of a brick's length, plus the inside layer of plaster. The brick is laid in Flemish bond. A handsome corbelled cornice formed by a row of bricks laid at an angle lies at the top of the front and back walls, in the shadow of the roof overhang. This decorative feature was also used on the old meetinghouse in the park. The window arches are flat. Some windows have stone lintels and sills.

No one knows now what kind of roof the building had in the beginning. No one knows if it had shutters in its early years. The Historic American Buildings Survey collected some photos of the building. One dating from

1940 and taken by Thomas T. Waterman shows white shutters with small diamond-shaped cutouts closed over all the windows. A 1934 photo by L.R. Winslow shows shutters only on the lower windows; these had quarter-moon cutouts. The recent maintenance work discarded the shutters.

We are also in the dark about much of the history of use of the building. After Richard Mendenhall died in 1851, it fell to his widow Mary and oldest daughter Minerva to manage the family property, including the Store House, as it was called. Minerva rented out the building during her lifetime, apparently.

When a new charter was given to Jamestown in 1859, measurement for the town boundary began at that intersection. The charter says that the brick storehouse "lately occupied by Nathan Gardner & Co." was there. The nature of Gardner's business is unknown.

In at least one instance, the building was rented out as a residence. In recent years, small shops have rented the space briefly.

When Minerva Mendenhall died in 1900, she left the "Brick Store House" and some other lots and buildings in the neighborhood to her niece, Gertrude W. Mendenhall. By 1928, it had become part of the twenty-five acres purchased by High Point that eventually became City Lake Park.

At that time, Mrs. Martha R. Tilden, Mrs. Eugene Armfield, Mrs. O.M. Bundy, Mrs. Manly Jones, Mrs. Hunt, Mrs. W.A. White and Mrs. William G. Ragsdale had formed a committee to plan a museum to be located in the building. When this was reported in the Greensboro *Daily News* on May 11, 1928, the building was referred to as a "house."

In the department of do-not-believe-everything-you-hear, it was reported that it was "opposite the old tavern where noted figures in history, including George Washington, are said to have stopped," and that "the house that will be available for a museum has portholes designed for use whenever the need for…defense might arise."

Well, High Point did develop a park, and a very nice one, but one without a museum. Thanks to that city for keeping these fine old buildings intact, and giving them a little TLC on occasion.

The Dam

When High Point turned forty in 1899, its officials undertook to improve its public water and sewer system.

Moving at municipal speed, they placed an order in 1901 for nine miles of pipe. In 1902, a small dam was built of brick and rock, which enclosed a small spring-fed reservoir. This reservoir was at the end of Pump Station

High Point City Lake was created when the dam (lower center) was built in 1928. Deep River flows south from the dam at the lower left, and is crossed by Main Street. City Lake Park lies on the left side of the river. *Courtesy City of High Point Parks and Recreation Department.*

Road, which runs east toward Deep River from Scientific Street, just south of the present-day Jamestown city limits. A powerhouse also was built to generate enough steam to drive two pumps.

In 1919, construction was started on a raw water-pumping station, which pumped water from a cofferdam on Deep River behind the station and forwarded it to the new Kearns plant in High Point. The old pond and treatment works were no longer needed and apparently were abandoned.

High Point's increased manufacturing in the booming 1920s dictated that still more water be found, though, so an elaborate plan was developed. William C. Olsen, a consulting civil engineer from Raleigh, was hired to oversee the project. The work moved forward at a good pace, considering all that was involved. The purchase of something over four hundred acres from about twenty landowners on both sides of both forks of Deep River had to be negotiated, and bids were solicited for the construction of a dam below the forks of Deep River at Jamestown. Creation of a reservoir, which would impound 1.5 billion gallons of water, was the goal.

The old High Point city reservoir on Pump Station Road was demolished about 2006. *Courtesy of the author.*

From among fourteen bids, the contract for the dam was awarded to the Grier Lowrance Construction Company of Statesville on November 12, 1926. The *High Point Enterprise* the following day reported the event with a subheading that said, in a wonderfully colorful and descriptive way, "Approximately $400,000 Involved In Three Contracts; Members of Council Decide Who Shall Have the Contracts Behind Closed Doors While Contractors Prance Up And Down the Hallway Protesting Vigorously Against Motive."

According to records of the High Point City Council minutes for 1926, the city acquired tracts from the following landowners: R.R. Ragan Goat Farm, D.W. Moore, J.A. Gardner, Edna Potter, H.A. Barnes, C.H. Mackay, Isaac McCollum, George T. Penny, J.L. Coltrane, R.R. Williams, the Methodist Protestant Orphanage, J.H. Ward and Edwin Long. In addition, there were four other tracts whose owners were not shown. One adjoined Barns, Garrett and Bevins; one adjoined R.R. Ragan and J.L. Coltrane; another adjoined Ragan and Potter; and another adjoined Mendenhall, Rush and Benbow. From Ed and wife Mary Steel, the city would need right of way for the pipeline. The Steels owned what is now the Mendenhall Plantation.

The dam was completed in 1928. High Point's water problems still plague Jamestown off and on.

Part IV

Gone But Not Forgotten

Some of these people and places we knew firsthand, and others we only wish we had known.

What Would Ole Jimmy Parsons Think?

James Parsons lived to the age of eighty-six, and during the later years of his life and for a generation or two afterward, those who knew him or knew of him referred to him as "Ole Jimmy Parsons." That's according to Jon Goodman, writing in the *Guilford Genealogist* (number eighty-three, 1998). Parsons died in 1857 and was buried at Ebenezer Methodist Church in Randolph County beside his first wife, Mary Fields, daughter of Joseph and Lydia (Julian) Fields.

However, his working life was spent as a millwright at the gristmill and sawmill he operated on Deep River, not far downstream from the mouth of Richland Creek, in the southern part of Jamestown Township. He also built a house near the top of the steep hill overlooking the mill.

Most people now refer to this site as Freeman Mill, and that's what it was beginning in 1862, a few years after Parsons's death, when John W. Freeman purchased the seven and three-quarters acres of the land that included the mill. A few years after that, James's second wife, Mary Barnard, moved to Indiana after selling additional land to Freeman, and that pretty well ended the Parsons family presence in the neighborhood.

The team that conducted the archaeological survey required by the National Historic Preservation Act of 1966 at sites of this kind determined that the earliest mention of a gristmill (and also a sawmill) here was in a 1793 deed showing that James Parsons bought the land from Jonathan Parker, who had bought it from George Parsons, who had bought it in 1787 from Timothy Barnard. So, exactly when the mill was originally built is open to speculation.

The Parson-Freeman Mill site on Groometown Road, with construction underway. The construction trailer at the upper left marks the site of James Parsons's house. The building on the right side of the road remains, marking the later Cummings property. The mill building was behind the trees and dirt piles on the left. *Courtesy Frederick P. Browning.*

Nora Parsons Fisher said that her great-grandfather James built in 1812 a gristmill and ten-foot-high stone dam that could be seen from his home overlooking the river. So, James may have rebuilt the original gristmill. Or, descendants may just have the dates wrong. The millstones were powered by a wooden undershot water wheel because the river gorge was so deep there. The original water wheel was fifty to sixty feet in diameter, she said.

The old foundation piers indicate the mill building was about twenty-five feet by fifty feet. They were still visible within the newer, larger foundation stones of the later mill.

"Parsons" is shown on the 1808 Price Strothers map of North Carolina. In 1815, Parsons was the tax collector for his district, which included a piece of present Sumner Township, as well as a big part of Jamestown. His list is a who's who of early history, including families named Osborn, Frazier, Wiley, Barnard, Coffin, Lane, Trotter, "Mash" (Marsh), Kersey, Leonard and so on.

Another Parsons descendant, Adin Baber, according to the Goodwin article, said that Parsons built a bridge in 1838 to accommodate customers on the east side of the river who could not cross his ford at flood stage. "J.P. 1838" was carved on one of the two thirty-foot stone piers, and Baber added that the state highway department capped them with concrete about 1931.

The study of the Freeman Mill site was done over a period of some months in 1997 and 1998 by a team composed of Loretta E. Lautzenheiser and her assistants of Coastal Carolina Resources, Inc.; John N. Lovett Jr., expert in old mills; and Jerry Leimenstoll, architectural historian. Their report, "Data Recovery at Freeman's Mill, Site 31GF373, Guilford County, N.C.," prepared for the Piedmont Triad Regional Water Authority, is filled with written descriptions and plentiful illustrations of what they found at the mill site. Many visits over several months gave the team experience with the variety of rainfall amounts affecting water flow at the mill. Hurricane Fran occurred during these months and submerged the turbines that were being studied.

From the road, the most visible relic of the mill was the kudzu-draped brick ruin of the two-story building of 1880. Built of handmade brick on a massive foundation of granite stones, it measured 101 feet by 50½ feet, and was twelve bays long and six bays deep. The hip roof, long gone now, is shown in a 1930s photograph that is included in the booklet. As a working woolen mill in its time, it held twelve looms, but went out of business before 1896 and converted to a gristmill. Problems with silt and the erratic water supply in Deep River ended that venture, and within a few years it was sold out of the Freeman family.

Other owners tried other uses for the mill, including ice plant and repair shop. At one point, it was converted to electric power. One later owner, T.C. Sheppard, lived in the nearby house on the west side of Groometown Road, across from the old Parsons house.

Old deeds of this area of Jamestown Township often refer to the "road to Parsons Mill," then later to "Parsons Mill Road." That became Freeman Mill Road, which, these days, goes nowhere near the old mill. Now, it's Groometown Road that passes it.

If the clock were turned back and "Ole Jimmy Parsons" could look from his doorstep down toward the earthmoving equipment that is steadily and noisily engaged in constructing a bridge high over Deep River, high enough to clear the waters of Randleman Lake, what would he make of it all? I think he, as a venturesome sort of fellow, with a practical sort of mind, might like it.

Freeman Mill Revisited

Freeman Mill, originally Parson's Mill, was the subject of my previous section, "What Would Ole Jimmy Parsons Think?" A few days after it was published, Doug Lee, of Winston-Salem, called to say he had an old picture of the mill. He would send a copy to me if I were interested in seeing it, and if I would see to it that the copy was placed in the Jamestown Alumni Archives. Of course I agreed and so it arrived in due course, and it is shown here.

Lee said that the photo was taken in the late '40s or early '50s, but he remembers going to the mill as early as the late '30s. At that time, a man named Cummins or Cummings used the old mill building, he said.

The Cummings home was at the top of the hill rising above the south bank of Deep River, and on the west side of present Groometown Road. The house on the east side of the road on the hilltop, right above the mill, was originally built by James Parsons, I believe, and then belonged to the Freemans after they purchased the mill. That house is no longer standing.

The Cummingses' connection with the old mill began in 1933. After being sold by the Freeman heirs in 1908 to M.T. Chilton and T.S. Groom, the mill was sold by Chilton, who had bought out his partner, to P.C. Sheppard. When Sheppard was unable to pay the taxes, it was sold at public auction to

Freeman Mill in the 1940s showed a history of uses in its attachments and alterations. *Courtesy Doug Lee.*

E.O. Cummings and J.C. Cummings in January 1933. During those years between 1908 and 1933, it is said that it had been a woolen textile mill. It would be interesting to learn more about that period.

At the time that Lee's photo was made, the Cummings operation in the old mill building consisted of a machinery repair shop and ice plant, he said. The tower on the left side of the building in the picture was the ice plant. Cummings and his partner or assistant built what was called a "Hoover Tractor" for the Lee family. The "tractor" was a converted Model A Ford automobile, and probably the Hoover Tractor moniker comes from a bit of Great Depression sarcasm. The mill building was abandoned in the 1950s, apparently.

For those interested in the old machinery that was in the mill, much of it was sent to the Museum of Power and Industry in Belvidere, Tennessee, and probably could be seen there. The museum is in the old Falls Mill, and Dr. John Lovett is the curator.

A photo taken by Fred Browning in November 2005 shows that most of the remaining shell of the old mill building had been taken down, leaving just one face. Now, it is gone, too. Work continues on the bridge over the river as the Randleman Dam project moves along.

Old Hickory Club Became a Boy Scout Camp

Most of us have heard of the Clarence Mackay estate, which was a hunting preserve of wooded lands that lay along the East Fork of Deep River, off Guilford College Road and north of Jamestown. The Mackay lodge was in what is now Cedarwood.

Not as many have heard of the Old Hickory Club, located between the Mackay property and Hickory Grove Church. Finding out exactly where it was and what happened to it required some detective work. This information came from the collection of Ragsdale papers at the Jamestown Alumni Archives.

The club was organized by a group of area businessmen who formed a corporation and sold the first shares in February 1921. At that time, a clubhouse and dam were under construction, and members were invited to visit the site and look it over, according to a notice sent out to shareholders by E.W. Freeze, president, and W.A. Ring, treasurer of the corporation.

Financial troubles plagued the project from the start, however, and building construction went faster than collection of delinquent dues. By June, the club secretary, W.C. Jones, was calling a meeting and sending out proxy forms so that the negotiation of a loan could be considered by the membership. The amount proposed was $200,000, which sounds like a lot of money to yours truly, and must have sounded like even more in 1922.

The formal clubhouse opening was announced for Wednesday evening, September 29, 1921, to be held from four until twelve o'clock, with dinner served at six and music for dancing beginning at nine o'clock, provided by the Elks Band and Orchestra.

Within the year, a new secretary, J.S. Pickett, was sending out a new meeting notice for June 8, 1922, proxies enclosed, with the bad news that the membership would have to consider their choices, which were described as reorganizing, finding additional capital, appointing a liquidating committee or applying for a court receiver to liquidate the assets of the club and dissolve the corporation.

On August 11, members received a letter from the club's committee, composed of O.A. Kirkman, C.C. Muse, C.A Barbee and High Point auctioneer J. Sib Burton, which notified them of the forthcoming sale of the Old Hickory Club. The property consisted of a fifty-three-acre farm, one eleven-room house and a four-acre lake stocked with black bass, bream, crappy and other game fish. It was just off the main road between Guilford College and Jamestown, near Hickory Grove Church and the hunting preserve and clubhouse of Clarence H. Mackay, and between the homes of Oscar Hassell and Jess Gardner. One paragraph in that letter makes the property sound like heaven on earth:

> *This is one of the best farms in Guilford County, surrounded by good roads with a number of beautiful springs and branches on it. The lake is one of the nicest to be found anywhere, and the clubhouse, built of pine logs standing upright and tongued and grooved together, is beautiful. There are 11 rooms in the house, a large dance hall, two bathrooms, and plenty of large closets. The furniture, consisting of beds, mattresses, chairs, tables, couches, cooking utensils, chinaware, swings, and rustic furniture, one steel range and other articles too numerous to mention will be sold. There is no prettier place in North Carolina for a summer home, country home, or club than this place. The house is built in a beautiful grove, about ¼ mile west of the Guilford College–Jamestown road.*

Sib Burton handled the auction of the property on August 14. W.G. Ragsdale, of Jamestown, purchased it. He had been one of the stockholders, and probably had taken an active part in the original organization. In fact, part of the original land had been purchased from other members of his family.

Old lodge, often called "Berlin Lodge," at the old Uhwarrie Boy Scout Camp. It fits the description of the building erected by the Old Hickory Club. *Courtesy Steve Bouldin.*

The described location sounds so much like old Camp Uwharrie, owned and used until about 1993 by the Boy Scouts, that that possibility was checked out at the courthouse—sure enough, that's just where it was. Although Women's College inquired about leasing the property, it was sold in July 1925 to C.L. Amos, H.B. Hiatt, J.E. Lambeth and J.O. Moffit, trustees, to be used as a Boy Scout camp.

Now the area is a neighborhood of beautiful and very expensive homes. But as long as the entrance road is named Akela Trail, that old hunting-fishing-camp-lodge flavor will be part of its ambience.

First Jamestown Public High School

Of all the photos in the collection of the Jamestown Alumni Archives, my favorite is the one dated 1911 and taken of the "High School Department" of Jamestown Public High School. In it, everyone is posed front and center for the camera, except for one young lady in the front row who is posed for a camera located somewhere over to the southwest.

She and her classmates might have been the first graduating class of the old high school that was built in 1907, one of only two rural public high schools built by Guilford County when high schools in the state "went public." Prior to this time, secondary education could be obtained only at private academies.

This high school was built at the site of Jamestown's old Flint Hill School, and very near (if not on) the site of the present United Methodist Church on Main Street. It is possible, but not certain, that this was the place where Hance Armfield established his academy in 1828 "near Jamestown." (Jamestown was at that time west of Deep River.) It was definitely the site of

This photo of the "High School Department" of Jamestown Public High School is dated 1911 and shows the class on the steps of the building that was built in 1907 and burned down in 1915. This was the first public high school in Jamestown. *Courtesy Jamestown Alumni Archives.*

Flint Hill Academy, which was at first Freemon's (or Freeman's) Male School, established by J.W. Freeman in 1859. Afterward, during the Civil War, Nereus Mendenhall kept Flint Hill Academy open, and it continued under other leadership and in different forms through the end of the century.

The first high school commission had three members: William G. Ragsdale Sr.; James R. Gordon, MD; and Daniel W. Moore. The school building cost $1,500, paid for by $500 in local tax money, matched by the county school board and matched again by the state. Lyndon Lea White was its first principal. There were thirty-one students—sixteen boys and fifteen girls. Two teachers were hired.

In 1907, the idea of publicly funded high schools was controversial. A sizeable part of the citizenry thought that children, especially those ages twelve and up, should be in the workforce. Many of them helped on the family farms and others, as young as eight, worked in cotton mills, and their small wages helped bolster family income. To mollify the opposition based upon traditional thinking, Jamestown's high school became an experimental "Farm Life School," where boys were taught agricultural skills on the school-owned farm and girls learned domestic sciences in special courses.

The school attracted a lot of students from the western part of the county, and many of them boarded at the school during the week. A dormitory was added, and then a second one—one for boys and one for girls. All of these buildings were two-story wooden frame structures with attics, large windows and high ceilings.

On February 18, 1915, the main building burned to the ground quickly. The cause of the fire was thought to be a defective flue. Fire apparatus from High Point was dispatched, but was too late to do much good. There were no injuries and students left the building in an orderly fashion. Space was appropriated here and there for classrooms to continue the school year.

In the meantime, the whole community, it seemed, became involved in building a new building. This one was of brick, designed by an architect, electrified and erected in record time on one of the old Farm Life School fields. When completed, the two dormitories were moved to stand behind it, and it opened in time for the next school year. It's still there, actually, showing its age, but doing pretty well.

As to the young lady in the photo, and all of the other boys and girls, identification of them would be welcome, and will be passed along to the Jamestown Alumni Archives for their records.

Menagerie and Circus Came to Town in 1842

The back pages of old issues of the Greensboro *Patriot* present advertisements for all sorts of things, from lost wallets to train schedules to lodge meetings. Reading them is a fine way to sample the various elements that made up the culture of Guilford County at any given time.

One ad that is more picturesque than most of its time is for the "Menagerie and Circus From the Bowery Amphitheatre, N.Y.," that appears in the *Patriot*'s March 22, 1842 issue. In a two-panel drawing, an equestrian circus act is depicted on the left, while two giraffes demonstrate the menagerie's presentation on the right. Below, it says, "The Proprietors most respectfully announce to the citizens of Greensborough that their unequalled troop of EQUESTRIANS and splendid CARAVAN OF WILD ANIMALS will be exhibited in Greensborough Wednesday, March 30th, 1842."

At the bottom of the ad, one of those pointing finger symbols so often used in old ads indicates that "the same will be exhibited at Jamestown, Tuesday, March 29."

In between the two statements the animals are named: elephant, kangaroo, black tiger ("the only one ever caged"), a specimen of the giraffe, African lioness, "the Great Pooner Bear of Hindoostan," Brazilian tiger, badger, black bear, pair of African gazelles, royal Bengal tiger, anaconda and boa constrictor, monkeys, birds, etc.

"The company of Equestrians, under the management of Mr. J. J. Nathans, are of first reputations in their different departments." The famed Indian Rubber Man, Mr. William Day, who had created much excitement wherever he had appeared, was to be on hand, and also others "in every department of the Olympic Exercises." An extensive band of musicians would accompany the performances with airs, marches, overtures and waltzes.

I wonder where they set up their show.

Since the circus was in Jamestown one day and Greensboro the next, we gather that it was moving south to north on the old Salisbury Road. (There was no railroad then.) We don't know where it crossed Deep River, but we have an account of how circuses did so when there was still a wooden covered bridge probably somewhere near the present bridge. The river was fairly deep at that time, just after the Civil War, because a dam had been built at the mill called Holton's (or Robbins's), where present Dillon Road crosses the river.

The old account was written by the late Miss Sophie Tilden of Jamestown and referred to information given her by her mother, Martha Robbins Tilden. She said the circuses traveled in slow processions, horses and elephants bringing

Circus advertisement from the 1842 Greensboro *Patriot*. The colorful advertisement noted that the circus would also perform in Jamestown. *Courtesy Greensboro* Patriot, *March 22, 1842.*

up the rear behind the wagons. "When they would reach the Jamestown bridge the elephants refused to cross. An elephant would put his foot on it, give the bridge a hard shake, and let out a loud bellow of protest."

There would be nothing for it but to lead the elephants down to the river and let them swim across. "The children in the community would run to the river to watch the elephants, and see them swim to the opposite bank." Well, I guess they would!

This old covered bridge is believed to have been swept away from its foundation about 1870, and it was replaced by an open bridge.

We in Jamestown can still see the circus train go through on its way to Greensboro each year if we are in the right place on the right spring day.

Union Hill School Will Be Back

It might be a surprise to you to learn that Union Hill Elementary School, that venerable landmark at the junction of Kivett Drive and Jackson Hill Road, is going to be demolished. It was a surprise to me. But a replacement, a new and improved building, has been on the planning schedule for some time.

Technically, Union Hill Elementary is in High Point, but it is so firmly connected to Jamestown that we have to claim it as one of our schools, too. In years past, hundreds of its graduating students moved on to attend Jamestown High School.

One of those was Madge Wilson Jester. She remembers when this school was built, in 1928. She had attended the earlier Union Hill School in a frame building that is now a residence on Jackson Lake Road, and she was very aware as the present Union Hill building was constructed on land purchased from her grandfather, E.S. Wilson Sr. In 1929, she attended classes at the new school. She recently found, and presented to the school, the photo made in 1929.

Mrs. Tammy Gruert, longtime media specialist and librarian at the school, has made this important event in the ongoing life of Union Hill Elementary an occasion for collecting its history. An astounding amount of stuff of all sorts has been stacked around her office in a corner of the school's library. Former students and teachers have responded with photos and newspaper clippings. School staff and faculty have looked through closets and cupboards for items that might have been stored away, and they've found scrapbooks and newsletters, among other items.

I confess I didn't examine this great stash too closely when I visited the school, but among the items I did read, my personal favorite is a little booklet entitled "Union Hill School Dedication Ceremony—September 25, 1983," published probably on the occasion of completion of extensive renovations to the old school. Most pages contain lists of dignitaries attending the event, and faculty and staff of the school.

Two pages in the back hold a "History of Union Hill" written by Ruby Allred, a retired teacher. There's a lot of information packed into these two pages. One of my questions—how did Union Hill get its name—was answered here: Mendenhall School, located on Hickory Chapel Drive, and Poore School, located near present Union Hill, joined with a school held in Kennett Friends Meetinghouse, at the present site of Oak Grove Baptist Church on Kivett Drive. This union of three small one-room schools was named accordingly. Both Mendenhall and Poore had been named for their former landowners. Allred's history also mentions nearby Haworth Springs and Triangle Lake, each of them popular picnic and recreation areas in their time. It also refers to the old gold mines that have defined this neighborhood since the early nineteenth century.

At Union Hill School, four classrooms and a cafeteria were added to the 1929 building in 1953. A second addition, to the left of the original structure as you face the building, held six classrooms and two other rooms. The third addition of a media center and five more classrooms was completed in 1965. Major renovation of the original building was done in 1983, when the old auditorium became the new library and other changes were made. To be honest, the building's interior seems a jumble to the first-time visitor, and taking all of these parts down and beginning again seems like a very good idea.

Union Hill School (1929–2008) will be replaced by a new one on the old site. *Courtesy Union Hill Elementary School.*

When opened, Union Hill had seven grades. The following year, grade eight was added, and it continued with grades seven and eight until 1966, when Jamestown Junior High School opened.

Now, kindergarten through grade five seem to fill all the available space.

And where will these kiddoes go next year while their old school is being dismantled? They will go to Allen Jay Middle School. And where will Allen Jay Middle School's kids go? They will go to Southwest Guilford Middle School.

The planning for this entire adventure has been extensive. On a certain day, boxes will be delivered to Union Hill so that faculty and staff can begin filling them with things that will have to be moved and that will fit in boxes. All furniture, books, office supplies, equipment, whatever, will be moved to Allen Jay. Everything should be ready by June 15. A new entrance to the school site from Central Avenue will enable some kinds of work to begin at one end of the site while the building is being torn down at the other end. No promises have been made, but lots of people hope that during demolition the decorative elements on the front façade of the building can be removed intact and added to the new building.

The next weeks will be very busy at Union Hill, and a high priority at the school is going to be keeping classes going as usual. Tammy Gruert is adding to her schedule the preparation of a PowerPoint program on the history of Union Hill that will be part of this year's closing events. Plus, she has to box up all those extra scrapbooks, photos, newspaper clippings and whatnot that will most certainly make the move to Allen Jay, and then back again to some new location in the new Union Hill Elementary School, scheduled to open within fourteen months.

Foscue House

Let's visit another part of the state, briefly. If you should be motoring along U.S. 17 south of New Bern, about when you reach a place named Pollacksville, you will pass a road sign directing your attention to the Foscue House on your left, which turns out to be an ancient, very handsome brick plantation house on the east side of the road.

"Hmmm," you may say to yourself. "Foscue. Why does that sound familiar?" That's what I did, anyway. "Something to do with Jamestown," I thought.

Of course I was right (as usual). There had been a Dr. Foscue in Jamestown, very fondly remembered years ago. He was connected with that fine old house in Pollacksville, North Carolina. I don't know how he came to be in Jamestown. However, it is a fact that in the summertime, Foscue relatives from "down east" would come to visit the doctor in Jamestown in order to get away from the heat and mosquitoes of Jones County.

That and a number of other facts about the family were learned by Jane Wade in 1975 when she wrote an article, "The Changing Face of Jamestown," for the *Farmer's Advocate*, published by the Historic Jamestown Society. At the time Jane wrote about him, the Foscue House in Jamestown was still standing at the corner of East Main Street and Gannaway.

Do you remember it? It was a big two-story place with a center entrance and one corner jutting forward just slightly, in a tower effect. There was a deep porch along the front and one side, and on the second floor a door opened out onto a little deck. There were ten rooms, each with a fireplace, large windows and high ceilings. The roof was of galvanized metal shingles, which never had to be replaced.

Dr. Foscue's office had its own entrance on the north side of the house. Mrs. Foscue, the former Vera Armfield, served as the doctor's assistant, as she had for her father, Dr. David Armfield, who had served as a Jamestown doctor for many years. Actually, Mrs. Foscue was herself a popular medical consultant who had a devoted following, even though she wasn't a doctor.

The house was built in 1909 by Jesse Johnson, and not a moment too soon, for the Foscues had three children by then and their fourth child was born either that year or the next. In addition to the children, space was needed in the house for Vera's brother, Eugene Armfield, who lived with the family, and also for the aforementioned Foscue family visitors who came each summer.

Dr. Foscue was practicing medicine in Jamestown during the great Spanish influenza epidemic that peaked in 1918. The epidemic began in Europe and spread rapidly through armies living and fighting in confined areas during World War I. It came home with troops and did its awful work throughout this country. There were few families in the United States that weren't touched by that epidemic, including many in Jamestown.

Dr. Foscue's death from a heart attack at the early age of forty-two is said to have been brought on by the stress and overwork that resulted from caring for flu patients. Vera Foscue, his widow, was called on for medical advice for years afterward, and she lived in the big old house until her death in 1968.

In 1975, the federal government purchased the old house, and in 1977, the new post office was dedicated and opened its doors (including the one now blocked) on the property. Bronze plaques in the post office lobby mention the Foscue House and the dedication date.

There was a good bit of pressure on the designers of the building to make it fit the "colonial" style, which was thought to be appropriate for Jamestown. I have always been puzzled by its orientation, since it just doesn't suit the space it was plunked down in. However, we're all used to

The Foscue House (1909–75) stood where the post office building is now. *Courtesy of the author.*

it now (except for newcomers who don't understand about the door that does not open).

A number of items from the Armfield and Foscue families are on display now on the stair landings in the Jamestown Public Library, and the upper floor honors them, as well. Large portraits of Dr. David Armfield and Phoebe Sapp Armfield are on the west landing, along with a roll-top desk. The east landing holds a large portrait of Dr. John E. Foscue and one of Vera Armfield Foscue, and a "lawyers" bookcase containing books and other items from the Foscue home. One of the items is the sketch of the old Foscue home shown in this section.

George E. Matthews Left Stories and Memories

All things aeronautical captured the public's fancy in 1930, and Jamestown was not immune.

In 1930, George E. Matthews, a forty-year-old auto mechanic with a year's worth of flying lessons behind him, took his Alexander Eaglerock biplane to 13,840 feet, nearly two and a half miles up, attempting to set a new altitude record. The attempt fell short by "a few feet," according to contemporary news reports, but it was a nice try and took one hour and forty-five minutes to accomplish.

The attempt was made at the Charles-Kenner Flying Service field. A consensus of early citizens' recollections is that there were two flying fields located between present Flowers Bakery and the Presbyterian Home, both of them off the south side the Greensboro–High Point Road, and so the exact location is not known. News accounts say C.L. Amos, of High Point, owned the field and flying service, and had been taking flying lessons at the field.

Matthews is still well remembered in Jamestown, and Coy Proctor and Winn Underhill both shared their recollections of him. Matthews owned and operated a garage, gas station and pool hall. His first garage was located where Jamestown Motor Company is now, and he later moved up the hill and built the station that now houses River Twist. It hasn't been that long ago, really, that two gas pumps stood at the edge of the street at 188 East Main.

According to the 1930 census, George Matthews, his wife Cora T., three daughters and George's father, Wirt J. Matthews, lived on the "Jamestown to Freeman Mill Rd." (I'm not sure what this is meant to be; maybe Oakdale Road.) Wirt Matthews, actually James W. Matthews, was an engineer at the sanatorium, another Matthews with an interest in things mechanical.

The altitude record event was well publicized in area newspapers, with Paul F. Davis, an Atlanta pilot recently hired as chief pilot of the Charles-Kenner Flying Service, as star of the show. On Sunday afternoon, June 22, at 2:30 p.m., as advertised, Davis began a long program of stunts. "He rolled, looped, did the tail spin, and then to make a perfect day of it, landed out of the sky with his motor turned off," the *High Point Enterprise* reported.

Then, at 4:00 p.m., George Matthews held all eyes as he circled, gaining altitude little by little, until the Alexander Eaglerock biplane looked no bigger than an English sparrow. The engine (a Curtis OX 5) could barely be heard from the field. It was hot on the ground, but "plenty cool up in the sky," the *Enterprise* said.

The crowd was estimated to be in the thousands. More exciting performances were planned for future Sunday afternoons. Air shows still draw large audiences, but at that time the novelty of it all must have added even more excitement.

No evidence was found that George had a career as a pilot, and it is possible that the Great Depression that turned a lot of ambitious dreams to dust can be held accountable for that. But he was flying high in experienced company on that day in June 1930.

Matthews's next most memorable exploit may have been the one he shared with Charlie Turner Sr., when Turner was the town manager and Matthews was the fire chief. The town purchased a (very) used fire truck from St. Louis, and George and Charlie drove it back to Jamestown. This was a long, cold, wet and windy trip, in a fire truck of such primitive design that the warning bell had to be rung with a rope.

There are more things that we don't know about George Matthews than things that we do know. But we are grateful for the interesting Jamestown stories all the same.

The Ragsdale Collection

There were three of us volunteers who met each week to list the contents of a dozen or so old-fashioned letter boxes filled with papers that had been given to the Jamestown Alumni Archives. The papers belonged to William Gannaway Ragsdale. The other members of the volunteer team were Linda Kenner, in charge of the archives, and Dot Perdue, treasurer of the Old Jamestown School Association. Later, Pat Koehler joined us. Descendants who wanted to see the papers preserved and made available to the public had donated the collection.

The job was about three-quarters tedious, but the rest was such a mix of unexpected information that it kept us all looking forward to the next tidbit. Among all those dreary bank statements and cancelled checks (usually filed under "W," for Wachovia) were many treasures.

Since Ragsdale's position as head of Oakdale Cotton Mill made him the major employer in this part of the county, as well as the de facto mayor in this unincorporated community, there were many letters from job seekers, most in pencil on lined paper. There's one from a woman whose husband was ill and unable to work, so she wanted to send her son to work at Oakdale Cotton Mill. There was a lot of correspondence relating to Ragsdale's appointment to operate Pomona Cotton Mill temporarily when it declared bankruptcy.

All sorts of business matters were attended to, with purchase of supplies and equipment for the mill heading the list. Eye-catching letterheads on some of the letters show suspiciously elaborate factories and warehouses, but then who could prove at this late date that the illustrations were slightly exaggerated?

Other contents related to sporting matters. There were advertisements, invoices and freight bills for goods such as shotguns and ammunition, and letters from friends and fishing guides referring to trips planned. There was a schedule for field trials to be held by an organization headed by Jay Gould, no less.

Automobiles purchased included a Reo and a Chalmers. Also, Mr. Ragsdale was a member of the Elks lodge. A chapter of the Junior Order of United American Mechanics was named for him. Politicians often sought his vote.

The reason the papers were offered to the Jamestown Alumni Archives was the number of school-related matters in the collection. Not only was Ragsdale active in the Jamestown School Committee, but he was also responsible for Oakdale School, which was built by the mill primarily for the use of mill employees. The present "old school"—the Jamestown Public Library—was built during the time these papers cover, and many details relating to its funding, design, construction and outfitting are revealed here. Some correspondence with teachers is included, one exchange expressing displeasure on the part of the domestic science teacher over the design of her school kitchen. There is a letter from the principal of Florence Colored School inviting Ragsdale to attend the closing exercises there. A number of school business letters are from Tom Faust, the county superintendent.

These were only the high spots. The plan was to make sure all of the school information was identified and photocopied. The originals of that material will stay in the archives. Copies, and the other material, will be handed over to another archival facility better prepared to deal with the larger quantity.

Part V

Making a Living

The first settler, James Mendenhall, was a miller. His gristmill continued in operation from the 1760s until 1926. Deep River provided the power for it, at first, and for many other small milling and manufacturing operations along its banks.

McCulloch Gold Mill

One of Jamestown's Halloween entertainment sites one year was Castle McCulloch on Kivett Drive, where the Greensboro Community Theater led visitors down the "Yellow Brick Road."

Some of those visitors probably remembered that the impressive 1832 building there was in ruins until 1985, when present owner Richard Harris began its restoration. Even as a relic of its former self, it was still arresting to glimpse it through the trees and undergrowth that had overtaken it.

Seeing the massive walls of cut stone blocks, the towering square chimney and, most of all, that twenty-foot Gothic arch at the south end of the building would simply stop you in your tracks on your first encounter and even on your second or third.

The site had passed from private ownership to Preservation North Carolina, which made it available for purchase and preservation, and then to Harris. Its historical credentials are as impressive as the building. It is on the National Register of Historic Places and the Historic American Engineering Record—listed on both, officially, as the "McCulloch Gold Mill."

Still known locally as the Rock Engine House sometimes, it stands at the center of what was once a busy and well-known mining district. A number of mines were located in this neighborhood during the years between about 1820 and the 1860s, and some of them changed ownership and names often. However, from the engineering record citation, it is known that during its operating lifetime this mill processed ore from the Lindsay Mine, Deep River Mine, Gardner Hill Mine and possibly the McCulloch Mine. In addition,

The McCulloch Gold Mill ruins photographed in 1977 by Randall Page. The Gothic arch is typical of buildings in Cornwall. *Courtesy Library of Congress, Prints and Photographs Division, Historic American Buildings Survey, Reproduction Number HABS, NC, 41-JAMTO. V.1-1.*

the study says, the mill probably crushed the ore of individual prospectors and miners.

It was built in 1832 by entrepreneur Charles McCulloch on Copper Creek property purchased from Robert Hodson. It is the only existing pre–Civil War engine house built solely as a gold mill in North Carolina. For architecture, McCulloch relied on a tried-and-true style seen in engine houses in Cornwall. For equipment, though, he turned to the latest technology. There was a new power source—the steam engine—and a new milling technique. McCulloch hoped that this would successfully solve the problem of how to extract gold from the hard quartz that came from fifty or more feet underground, because by the 1830s, the easily accessible gold had already been mined.

He installed a steam engine, probably of the walking beam type, and a Chilean mill, perhaps two, of fourteen-foot diameter, twice the normal size. There was also a retort to recover the mercury or quicksilver used in separating the gold from the rock.

The massive building wasn't all of the operation, of course. When the studies of the site were made by various teams, they were hampered by trees that had been planted in the 1940s for harvest, but they did find that there

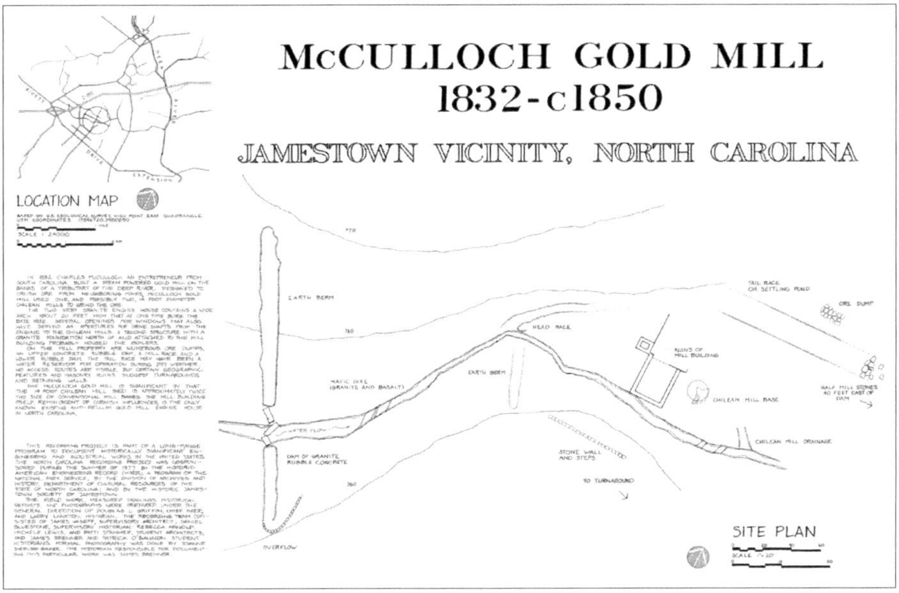

Site plan of McCulloch Gold Mill, 1832 to circa 1850, as delineated by Michele Lewis, 1977, revised by Richard K. Anderson, 1978, in the Historic American Buildings Survey of 1977. *Courtesy Library of Congress, Prints and Photographs Division, Historic American Buildings Survey, Reproduction Number HABS, NC, 41-JAMTO.V.1.*

had been a rubble-masonry dam about 260 feet upstream from the building, flanked by earthen dikes 210 feet long, and a sixteen-inch sluice gate that let water flow into the headrace. Also, there were traces of the millrace, a lower rubble dam, ore dumps and roads. The race diverted the stream and also directed water from the dam behind the mill building and into a tailrace, which was probably also a settling pond. The race provided water for the boilers, and also, by way of sluices, to the Chilean mills for the crushing work. This water then flowed back into the original streambed.

Those who wrote the citation for the Historic American Engineering Record, surely the best able to understand the workings of the Rock Engine House, found many things about the site and the building "bewildering," probably in that important elements were missing or were unusual. The report concentrates on the technical aspects of the whole site. It is a full and interesting record of what was seen at the time, about 1980.

The National Register citation provides more detail on the architecture. Copies of both citations can be found in the vertical files of the High Point Public Library's North Carolina Collection.

The First Jamestown Gold Miners

If you are curious about old mines near Jamestown, any fellow who spent his school years in Jamestown can probably show you at least one (though one of my sons, who does not know of any, disagrees). These places are dangerous, and locations are pretty well disguised now, but boys pass this knowledge on from one to the next. Those of us who were not Jamestown schoolboys either have to find a guide or settle for reading about the mines.

The *Guilford County Atlas*, published in 1976 by the county commissioners, shows five mine sites in Jamestown Township. First is Gardner Hill Mine, located on the east side of Reddicks Creek, north of Wiley Davis Road, and probably in Grandover now. Then there is a row of three—Jack's Hill Mine, North State Mine and Lindsay Mine—between Harvey Road and Kivett Drive spaced along between S.R. 1354 and Riverdale. The last one is Gold King Mine, not precisely placed, but lying east of Groometown Road, north of Deep River and near the Sumner Township line. These reflect the names reported in the 1887 Geological Report of North Carolina, under the title of *Ores of North Carolina*, by W.C. Kerr and Geo. B. Hanna.

The first reported gold discovery in North Carolina was in 1799, when John Reed found the mineral at what is now known as the Reed Gold Mine north of Charlotte. This, of course, set off a search for more of the wondrous stuff, and at some time before 1819, gold had been discovered on William Hodson's property near Deep River in Guilford County. We know this because an agreement between William Hodson and Edward Poor, dated January 25, 1819, was recorded with the county register of deeds, stating that Poor was entitled to "work & use wood & water in working a gold mine on the land of said William." Poor had posted a bond of $5,000 and was to pay Hodson one-fourth part of the gold or metal recovered.

Edward Poor was successful enough during the next few years to cause the honorary title of "Captain" to be placed on this tombstone. He died in 1827, and was buried in Old Union graveyard, also called Holton-Vickrey cemetery, on River Road. A number of deeds, including the agreement with Hodson mentioned above, were recorded following his death as part of his estate settlement. These records give the distinct impression that Edward Poor was a wheeler-dealer, a man with gold fever. His various tracts shared boundary lines with Robert Hodson and Jesse Field.

William Hodson (or Hodgson), mentioned above, came from a sizeable tribe of the name. Another member was Robert W. Hodson, who also owned one of the earliest mines. In his later years, Robert wrote about mining in the period between 1825 and 1831. In an article in the *Guilford*

Genealogist (number twenty-nine), Jack Perdue quoted from this 1879 letter from Robert to a Guilford County cousin, Philip Horney Hodson. Robert had moved to Indiana in 1831. The letter said, in part:

> *I think in the year 1825 my brother Jeremiah and I in prospecting along a branch found some particles of gold by washing the sand in a pan (a little previous I think some particles had been found on John Teague's land near by on another branch, perhaps by Wm. Jessup, which was afterwards known as the Horney Mine.) From some knowledge of the geological stratas of the earth we coursed the vein over the high land to the next branch, thence up the hill some distance, where a ledge of quartz jutted out, not more than a foot thick, leading S.S.W., the general course of ledges of rock in that section of the country. We found some particles of gold in quartz. After harvest that summer my brother and I commenced sinking a pit on the hill. We went perhaps 15 or 18 feet deep, looking for larger pieces of gold than are generally found in the veins, but finding none then gave up the pursuit till next summer.*

The letter says that Robert read all he could about geology, mineralogy and metallurgy "from the best books, papers, men, etc., in my reach." Then they went back to work, following the vein of quartz, washing the ore, crushing it in mortars, grinding it and then washing it with mercury.

"The gold in the ore was pure," he continued, "but there was sulphates of various metals combined in the ore. When we succeeded in the work, it produced a wonderful excitement. Men came from far and near, went to work sinking shafts at random and getting no pay."

Robert also mentioned again the Horney Mine (location not stated), saying that it opened soon afterward and was moderately successful, as were other places in Guilford and Randolph. They were worked for gold, but copper was plentiful in some of the mines.

The Hodsons worked at their mine for about four years, finding some very rich small pockets:

> *Some days we did not make more than $1.00 to the hand, other days much more. The largest day's work we ever done, was to dig out the ore, haul it to the washing place and wash out a little over $90.00, or $30.00 to the hand. We only went a little over fifty feet deep while I worked the vein. The vein thickened from near a foot on the surface to near five feet in the bottom. We sold out, I think, in the Spring of 1831 to Andrew Lindsey, James Robbins and Jesse Shelly.*

According to Fred Hughes's book *Guilford County, N.C., A Map Supplement*, F.W. Davis built a dam and geared mill at the present site of Oakdale Cotton Mill in 1826, the purpose being to power a gristmill, sawmill and pounding works.

In 1833, the heirs of Edward Poor sold mineral rights on a tract that Edward had sold to Isaac Person. Purchasing those mineral rights was Charles McCulloch. This was the same Charles McCulloch who built the rock engine house on Copper Creek on property purchased from Robert Hodson.

As it turned out, that was only the beginning.

Lindsay Mine

The Lindsay of the Lindsay Mine was Andrew Lindsay, although during his time it was called the Guilford Gold Mining Company, and it was one of the two gold mines granted charters in 1831 in Guilford County, the earliest chartered mines in the county. Andrew Lindsay, James Robbins and Jesse Shelly formed the company when they purchased the business from brothers Robert W. and Jeremiah Hodgin.

Andrew Lindsay was one of the sons of Robert and Ann (McGee) Lindsay. His youngest brother, David, lived in Jamestown and was a storekeeper and postmaster, but Andrew lived near the original Lindsay homeplace on Haw River near the Forsyth County line. He bought hundreds of acres of land here and there, however, and many of those, as well as his Guilford Gold Mining Company shares, were still among many other investment properties mentioned in his last will and testament. His wife and daughters each received shares in the gold company (along with other property). In addition he owned a tract "below the Gold Mill" that he referred to as the "Poor Tract." I didn't trace this land, but it probably belonged to early miner Edward Poor.

When Andrew died in 1844, it was during an active period for the local mines. McCulloch's gold mill was up and running and moderately successful in extracting gold. The steam engines were a marvel at producing power. The great discoveries of gold in California were still a few years in the future, so North Carolina, with its small and scattered mines, was still an attractive target for investors.

I won't try to account for all of the transactions that involved Lindsay's holdings and connections with mining, involving sale of mineral rights in some cases, as well as outright sales of land. However, Dr. Shubal G. Coffin of Jamestown, who dabbled in properties and assorted other ventures, purchased the Guilford Gold Mining Company from its then president, Jesse Shelly, and sold it to a group of investors headed by John L. Colby. There were at least two tracts of land involved, one described as being on Bull Run, of more than 800 acres, and one of 155 acres. This company then was incorporated in the "City, County and State of New York" by Colby and the other investors, all of New York, as the Lindsay Mining Company. The sale occurred in 1853, and the incorporation probably soon afterward.

Consistently reserved in the deeds for the smaller tract of 155 acres was a small piece (28 acres?) held for Jeremiah "Hodson," and then later, for Sarah Hodson.

The demise of the Lindsay Mining Company came in 1855, when the Bank of Cape Fear and thirty-nine other creditors forced a sale of the company. It was advertised to be held in May 1855.

A number of other mine bankruptcies also occurred in 1855, probably a result of the major gold discoveries elsewhere and of the dangers of speculation.

Many Miners Followed the Gold

Immigrants are nothing new in Jamestown. Of course we recognize that all of our families—with extremely rare exceptions—began with immigrant ancestors, so we'll skip over that patch of common wisdom. What we're talking about here are "foreign-born" residents.

In 1850, there was a real count of the foreign-born residents when the federal census was taken. In Guilford County, we were very fortunate to have "marshals" (census takers) who wrote down the counties of birth of each resident, as well as the states and also the countries, if other than our own. No towns are identified on this census, but I used my best judgment to set off what I thought was about right for the Jamestown area. Here's what I found:

John Forescu, thirty-five, born in Ireland, was a laborer living in Richard Mendenhall's household. Lewis Clark, fifty-three, was a laborer born in England, living in the Will Jackson household, probably somewhere in old Jamestown.

John B. Gluyas, twenty-six, was born in Cornwall and was a tanner who had a six-month-old baby, James M., in his household. I believe he lived in the Florence area. Mildred R. Gluyas, daughter of James and Miriam Mendenhall, who died in May 1850 and is buried at Deep River Friends Meeting, was John's first wife. He married Lydia (Hunt) Couch in 1853.

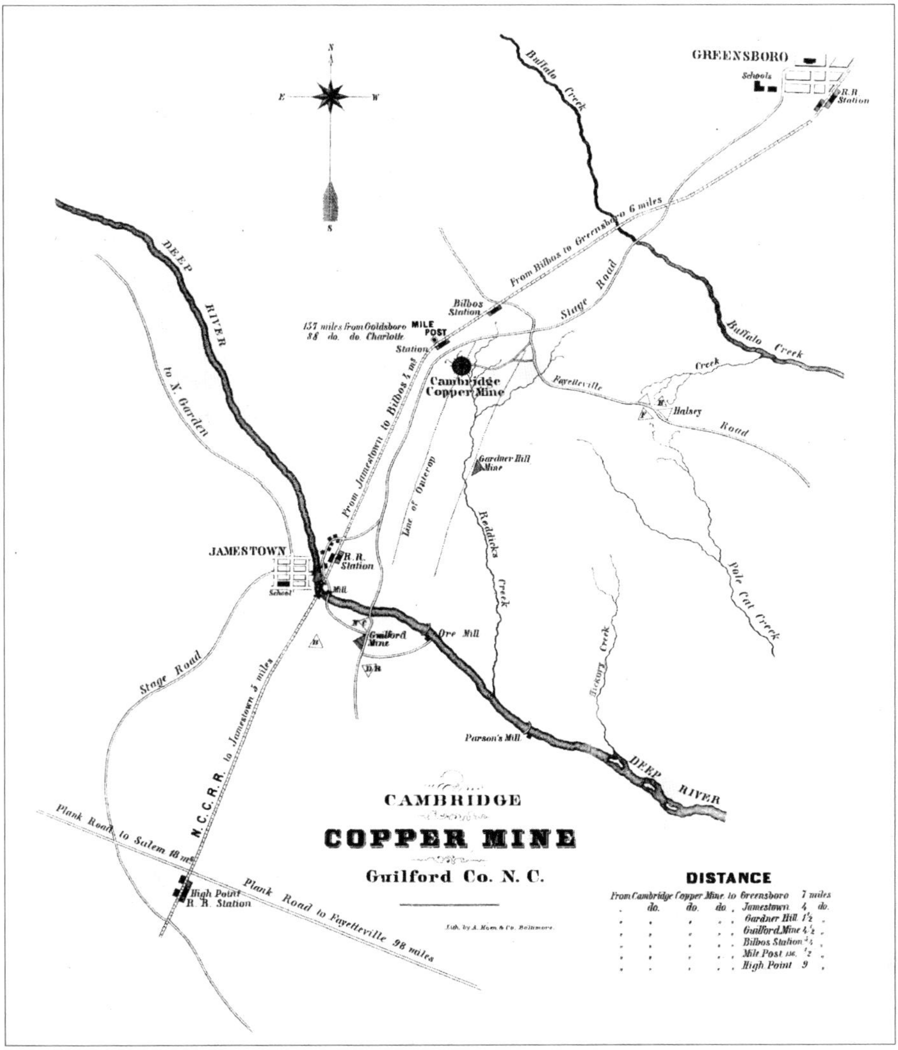

Copper mine map from a prospectus for the Cambridge Copper Mine shows Jamestown, the Gardner Hill Mine and other local landmarks. *Courtesy Greensboro Historical Museum Archives.*

An older John Gluyas lived near the gold mill, perhaps, or near one of the mines, next to Stephanus Kersey, who was a "gold washer." Gluyas was an engineer, born in Cornwall, England, age fifty-four, with a wife Mary, forty-nine, who was also born in Cornwall. Mary was living with a William Gluyas, twenty-eight, in Randolph County in 1860. There was no mention of John.

Two more Cornwall-born miners, John Hoskins, forty-three, and John Hammond, thirty-six, were in what appears to be the gold mine area southeast of Jamestown in 1850. So was William Gribble, thirty-two, whose children's birthplaces give us a map of the family's trek. William, thirty-two, and Jane, his wife, thirty, were born in Cornwall, and so was their son John, nine. However, their daughter Eliza, five, was born in Rowan County, North Carolina.

Living fairly close together were Thomas Moore, thirty-one, born in Cornwall; Samuel Stephens, twenty-nine, with wife Elizabeth, nineteen, both born in Westmoreland, England; and James Truoram, twenty-nine, and wife Mary, twenty-five, both born in Cornwall. All three of these men gave their occupation as "miner." Also in this area was a rarity, Frederick Miller, a gardener, born in Hanover, Germany.

Living near the mines was John Eudy, thirty-four, another miner born in Cornwall. His wife, Mary, twenty-five, and oldest child were both born in Shenandoah, Virginia, while a young son was born in Guilford. By 1860, John Eudy was listed as "Supt. of Mines," and in addition to his own family there are forty other miscellaneous names shown in his household, plus, at the end of the list, four more Eudys. This must represent the Gardner Hill mining camp or village, because Eudy worked for that mine. Among the group are five English-born, in addition to John. In 1880, Eudy is once again simply a "miner," probably because the mines were largely played out by then and no one was hiring superintendents.

Family Search shows a pedigree chart for John Eudy that indicates that he died in 1897 in Henderson (County), North Carolina. One of the things the Henderson County area was famous for in the late nineteenth century was the discovery of the mineral zirconia. His father, Alexander Eudy, born in Cornwall, England, died in Dutch Flats, Grass Valley, Placer County, California. His mother, Mary Ann Gribble, born in Cornwall, died in Thomasville, Davidson County, North Carolina, in 1869.

I wonder how many of the other Jamestown miners of 1850 had the kind of gold fever that leads them on and on. It would be interesting to follow them all, to see how many ended up in Cripple Creek or Placerville—or Henderson County.

Gardner Hill Mine

One of the best-known mines near Jamestown was the Gardner Hill Mine, located three miles east of town, near Reddicks Creek. For many years, the remains of a timber framework over the mine shaft marked the spot.

Public Laws of North Carolina for 1854–55 show that Gardner Hill Mining Company was chartered by the general assembly during that session. Officers of the corporation were A.S. Harvey, James F. Jordan, James E. Hoyt, S.P. Allen, Frederick Grist and George H. Brown. Several other mines were incorporated at the same time: Guilford Gold & Copper Mining Company, McCulloch Gold Mining Company, Hodgin Hill Mining Company and Fisher's Hill Mining Company.

In an 1887 publication, *Ores of North Carolina*, written by W.C. Kerr and Geo. B. Hanna, it was reported as a copper mine with three veins, one of which had been worked to a depth of 100 feet. A report published in 1896 said of the then-abandoned mine that it had five vertical shafts, one of 258 feet, as well as the Creek shaft of 100 feet; the Underlay shaft, 175 feet; the Old Engine shaft on the south end of the property, 175 feet; and the White Oak shaft, 150 feet deep.

When J.W. Cannon wrote an article about the Gardner Hill operation for the Greensboro *Daily News* in December 1931, the ruins of the old workings were still visible. His article is accompanied by a photo of a "tower" that was "erected over a vertical shaft which goes into the earth 258 feet and from which lead a maze of tunnels that spread out along a vein for more that 5,000 feet."

Cannon had access to a mine record book from 1859 to 1860 in the possession of Martha Robbins Tilden, who told Cannon she had rescued it from a fire. It records payments of $192.50 for the hire of twenty-eight slaves to work in the mine during the month of June 1861. The payments were made to W.A. Caldwell, acting as an administrator.

The mine was abandoned soon after the Civil War, according to Cannon, and old machinery and twenty-five thousand tons of ore were left scattered around the shafts. Some of that debris was still there in 1931.

John Eudy, a Cornish immigrant, had been a superintendent at both the Gardner Hill and the Clegg mines. Fred Hughes, in *Guilford County, N.C., A Map Supplement*, names others who were later employees of Clegg Copper, including two Eudys, Henry and William, probably sons of John.

Hughes wrote that the gold mining industry was supplanted by copper mining beginning in the 1850s, and this affected the Gardner Hill as well as other mines. The Clegg Mining Company operated successfully in the old Gardner Hill site into the 1870s. Developing around the mine were a company store, a school (Blackjack School, I believe) and a church.

Familiar Jamestown names associated with the Gardner Hill site included John Farrington, a miner and customer at the company store; James Palmer, commissary bookkeeper; John Wicker, mule team driver; and Rebecca Dean, ore picker. Women, it is said, did not go into the mine, but were hired for other work topside.

The store was at one time managed by William Millis Wiley, and sold a wide variety of goods. Wiley, who was also a schoolteacher and legislator, lived in what is now called the Gardner-Wiley House. The house and the mine were on the same tract of land purchased by William's father, Shannon Wiley, in 1856, and they still seem linked together, even if only in an unofficial way.

One final note: the Greensboro *Daily News* of August 24, 1952, reported that Miss Dorothy Dillard of Sedgefield received the title of the Gardner Hill Mine as a gift from her parents when she graduated from high school in Greensboro. Among the papers she received was a copy of a secret map drawn up by John Eudy showing where gold ore had been stored within the mine when it was being mined only for copper.

Lots of folks believe, as Mrs. Alverdia McGeehee Allred was quoted as saying in the Greensboro *Daily News* article, that "the old timers only raked the top off" of rich mineral deposits near Jamestown.

Prospecting is still a popular pastime for the local diehard gold seekers.

Gibson Park Honors the Jamestown Rifle

Gibson Park is on the south side of Wendover Avenue, just east of Premier Drive. Its eastern boundary follows what in old parlance would be called the "meanders" of the East Fork of Deep River. If you take the entrance road south as far as it goes, past the soccer and ball fields and Twin Ponds Trail head, you reach a parking lot, playground and the old Deep River Cabin.

Near the cabin is the path that connects to the Bicentennial Greenway, which also follows the "meanders" of the river, just as an old trail or road did. A planner with Guilford County Community & Economic Development says that when he first walked over the ground, when the park and parkway were in the planning stages, that trail could be seen plainly as it lay along the course of the river. The trail became part of the Bicentennial Greenway, paved now, to the dismay of preservationists.

At the head of that connector path in the park is a handsome bronze plaque, headed "Jamestown Rifle." It lists eighty-two known gunsmiths and apprentices who once practiced their craft in the Jamestown area, primarily along this watercourse—East Fork, Long Branch and also Bull Run—which supplied power for their shops. The Colonel John Sloan Camp, Sons of Confederate Veterans Camp #1290, placed the plaque there on May 10, 1994.

A rifle was a necessary piece of equipment for eighteenth- and nineteenth-century residents of Guilford County, but it wasn't the sort of thing that just

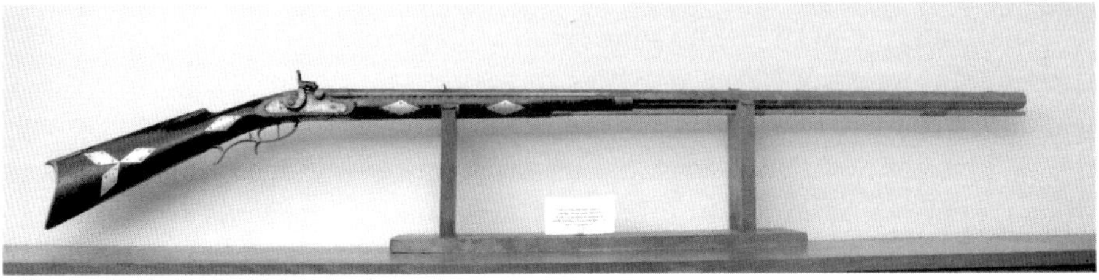

Jamestown rifle made by a member of the Lamb family on display at the Friends Historical Collection at Guilford College. Other examples of the Jamestown rifle can be seen at the Greensboro Historical Museum and the High Point Historical Museum. *Courtesy Friends Historical Collection, Guilford College, Greensboro, North Carolina.*

anybody could whip up. It needed expertise. It is not surprising that the ones made around Jamestown resembled the long rifles made in Pennsylvania that had been brought into this area by the first white settlers. It is a style often called the Kentucky rifle. The Jamestown gun makers were a close-knit group and of course developed certain local characteristics. Their guns were slender, graceful, muzzleloading rifles.

H. Clay Briggs, a native of the Florence community, wrote about them in 1935, based upon personal knowledge of his neighbors and the neighborhood. His article may have been in a newspaper, but is also among Deep River Friends Meeting's papers. Jack L. Perdue, of Jamestown, kept a continuously updated, carefully documented report on his ongoing research into the rifles and gunsmiths until his death, and, to my knowledge, it is the most complete work on the subject. There is a copy of this booklet, *The Gunmakers of Jamestown*, in the North Carolina Collection at the High Point Library. Also, the High Point Museum has a substantial collection of Jamestown Rifles.

One of the earliest known gun makers was Thaddeus Gardner (1774–1848), who was advertising his wares in a Charlotte newspaper as early as 1836. His shop was on Gallimore Dairy Road, and in a manufacturing census taken in 1850, the shop listed an annual production of one hundred "rifle guns."

Nearby was the first shop of William Lamb, born in 1806, probably a kinsman of Gardner, and known to have worked with him. Lamb, generally known in later years as "Captain Billy," apparently worked with several partners and in several locations over the years, but never far away from the East Fork. Briggs said that, after the Civil War, and as old age caught up, Captain Billy set up a small shop on what is now East Fork Road, where he made rifle triggers for S.H. Ward, a later and prominent gun maker.

The district where rifle manufacturing shops have been identified stretches from Gallimore Dairy Road south to Oakdale Cotton Mill, where arms were manufactured during the Civil War, and from a line on the west formed by Penny Road and Highway 68, where Henry Ledbetter and Nathan Wright worked, to the present Adams Farm area, where Jabez Stevens and Ithamer Armfield were located. Most were small operations by today's standards, in modest log buildings, employing a few people here and a few people there, but all skilled artisans—or learning to be.

Though no one knows when the first rifle was made here, Perdue was probably correct in saying that the period of production spanned the one hundred years of the nineteenth century.

They not only made them, but the gun makers tested them and became good marksmen. You may have heard this story, but it is a good one. H. Clay Briggs wrote it this way:

> *It has been told that Capt. Billy Lamb was out one day preparing to shoot a squirrel. The squirrel peeped around a limb and asked, "Is your name Lamb?" Capt. Billy answered, "Yes." The squirrel inquired again, "Capt. Billy Lamb?" Upon receiving an affirmative reply again, the squirrel said, "Then don't shoot. I'll come down."*

Florence Armory

Most of Jamestown's Civil War buffs know about the armory that was located near present East Fork Road in the community of Florence. It is well advertised by a sign near the road's junction with Penny Road where in 1989 the Colonel John Sloan Camp of Sons of Confederate Veterans erected a sign stating "North Carolina Armory at Florence." Fewer people know, however, that its commander, Captain Z.S. Coffin, was a local man.

Zimri Smith Coffin was born in 1833 on the family farm of his parents, Abner and Rachel (Osborn) Coffin, located along the southeast bank of Deep River south of present Kivett Drive. Interstate 85 now angles across this tract of land that was a 1787 state grant to Zimri's great-grandfather, Nantucket Quaker Peter Coffin. The property was passed down to Peter's son Joseph Coffin and then to Joseph's son Abner. As did many other descendants of Quaker settlers, Abner and his children became Methodists. There were nine children in the family, seven of whom survived to adulthood.

His friend Braxton Craven, then president of Trinity College in nearby Randolph County, referred to Zimri in 1853 as "a photographer." Jerome

Dowd's book *Life of Braxton Craven* describes a trip made to Philadelphia by Craven, his wife and Zimri Coffin. The group was entertained before leaving by Dr. Shubal G. Coffin of Jamestown. Dr. Coffin and Zimri were some kind of cousins, related but not closely.

According to a biographical sketch of Zimri in *Memoirs of Georgia Historical and Biographical*, Vol. II, published in Atlanta in 1895, he attended dentistry lectures at Pennsylvania College in Philadelphia, completing them in 1857. He soon afterward located in New Bern, North Carolina, where he opened a dentistry practice and remained until the beginning of the Civil War. The census taken in 1860 shows that he was a dentist and was living in a hotel in New Bern.

As New Bern was well within North Carolina's sound area, it was among the first targets of the North when Civil War hostilities began. The city was captured on March 14, 1862.

The only service record I have found for Z.S. Coffin lists his unit as "Ord. Dept of N.O." (which I think should probably read "N.C.") and his rank as "Captain and Agent." So I cannot say when and where he was inducted into Confederate service. It seems clear that he headed back home, though.

C. Michael Briggs's booklet *The Longrifle Makers of Guilford County: The History of the Jamestown Rifle* says that the Florence Armory was created in 1861, and it indicates that the establishment was in business by December of that year, its business being adapting "Country Rifles" for military use. Between December 1861 and April 1862, according to Briggs, 461 civilian rifles were rebored to fire .50-caliber balls. The armory also took parts from other contractors and assembled rifles. The Greensboro Historical Museum has a display showing how those rifles were made.

On April 11, 1865, says Briggs, the Florence Armory was burned by a group of men of the Fifteenth Pennsylvania Cavalry, led by Captain Adam Kramer. Kramer claimed that they destroyed 800 completed rifles and 2,500 partially completed ones.

Zimri Smith Coffin began to trade in commodities and stocks after the war, according to his biographical sketch. He cleared $10,000 in one year, and went to Georgia to invest his gains in the timber business. This failed and he went back to dentistry, settling in Stewart County, where he married and gradually added farming, a mercantile business, milling and other commercial interests to his life. He served a term in the state legislature in 1880–81.

I wonder if he left any interesting photos of Jamestown to his descendants.

Beard's Hat Shop

All that recent work with heavy equipment to clear and grade the old Wrenn Farm property just east of Flowers Bakery has tipped the old Beard's Hat Shop sign off true vertical in recent weeks. But it is still upright, and still the oldest sign of its kind around Jamestown.

Under "Beard's Hat Shop," it proclaims, "William Beard made & sold hats at his well-known shop, established before 1795 and later operated by his son David. Site 1 1/3 mi. N."

This is one of the highway historical markers placed by the North Carolina Highway Historical Marker Advisory Committee, at least under that group's authority, to mark places of interest along the state's roads. The project began in 1936, and this sign, which is J19, was put up in that year. It is unusual in that it marks the site of a business establishment.

The actual location of Beard's Hat Shop one and one-third miles north was in what is now the Meadows of Jamestown development on the east side of Penny Road, and is probably near the northeastern section of Queen's Grant Road. In 1996, when the development was being prepared as a building site, it was still possible to locate old bricks, as well as two vats that were once fed by a spring and were part of Beard's tan yard.

Beard's Hat Shop photographed in the 1870s. It was built on land that David Beard purchased in 1797 and continued as a business until Beard's death in 1849, and for a few years afterward. *Courtesy Friends Historical Collection, Guilford College, Greensboro, North Carolina.*

The tract of land where the hat shop stood was purchased by Beard from Phineas Mendenhall, a son of James Mendenhall (who built the mill just down the road, and for whom Jamestown was named). David built his hat shop of brick, and also a large house, which was about two hundred yards east of the shop. David had inherited his "interest in his hat makers trade, and also the hatter's tools" from his father, William Beard.

William Beard's land was just south of Deep River Meeting on the south side of what is now Wendover Avenue That old house stood for many years until burning down in 1993. The large Beard family was a substantial presence in the Deep River neighborhood from about 1790 until the 1840s and 1850s, when many of the family members moved to the Midwest.

David continued the hat business established by his father, and tried to add to it by importing a large and expensive stock of general merchandise at the beginning of the War of 1812. This was a serious miscalculation of the effect of the war on Beard's part, however, and the depression that followed that war nearly wiped him out. He returned to just making hats and farming, and passed the rest of his life in that way. He died in 1849.

In the Friends Historical Collection at Guilford College, there is a large hat of the type that Beard probably produced. It was made from the hide of a beaver. Beard's stock of beaver pelts probably came from local citizens who trapped them along Deep River and its tributary creeks and sold them to Beard or traded them for new hats.

Beard's hats were said to have been famous as far west as Indiana, where many local Quakers had moved from this area, and from where they sent orders back to Beard. The hats were further made famous by a children's book by Mabel Leigh Hunt, *Benjie's Hat*, which told how a little boy, Benjie, lost his hats, and how his grandmother gave Beard one pig and two and a half bushels of turnips to make a new one for the boy. You can still read that book at the Jamestown Public Library, where it is an important part of its collection.

Benjie's Hat

I will confess right here and now that I had not personally read *Benjie's Hat*. But I had heard about it for years through genealogical research, believe it or not. Over the years, I have conducted genealogical research in Guilford County records for many descendants who left Guilford County for points west. Many of these folks went to Indiana, and more than one of those descendants told me that *Benjie's Hat* was one of their resources for general

Benjie's Hat on display at the Jamestown Public Library. *Courtesy of the author.*

information about Guilford County, its famous Beard's Hat Shop, Guilford Battleground, Jamestown and Dobson's Crossroads (which turns out to be Kernersville).

Benjie's Hat was written by Mabel Leigh Hunt, illustrated by Grace Paull and published by the F.A. Stokes Company in 1938. Hunt was a librarian in the children's department of the Indianapolis library and was related to some of the old Quaker families of Guilford County. Her book is, as mentioned, a book for children, which means that most surviving copies are going to be pretty beat up, and it apparently has not been reprinted. There are three copies in the Quaker Collection at Guilford College, but I do not see copies listed in either High Point's or Greensboro's public libraries.

The summary of the contents says that it is about a young Quaker boy, Benjie, who loses or ruins his good hats and must put up with makeshift ones until he signs a contract in order to get a wonderful new hat made especially for him.

This is where Beard's Hat Shop comes in, the real place in the made-up story, where people from the Midwest, especially Indiana, really did send orders for hats because it was so well known during the period from about 1800 until about 1849.

According to a newspaper article of 1961, the fictional Benjie was modeled after the real William Hussey Idol (1847–1930), who did have a real hat from Beard's and whose daughter, Pearl, was one of Mabel Leigh Hunt's guides when the author visited the Deep River area before writing the book.

Those of you who like to collect old Jamestown stuff might keep an eye peeled for a nice old copy of *Benjie's Hat* and add it to your collection.

Thomas Cook, First Manager of Oakdale Mill

To men of business in the nineteenth century, the pocket diary was an indispensable tool for leading an orderly and successful life.

We turned up two at Oakdale Cotton Mill that had belonged to Thomas H. Cook, the first superintendent of Logan Factory, which later became Oakdale Cotton Mill. With the diaries was a typed transcript of others. More recently, seven were given to the Jamestown Alumni Archives by Emily Ragsdale. Altogether they cover the period of June 1865 to March 1876.

However, there is a major gap in the record they present that goes from December 25, 1865, until June 1870. Surely Cook kept up the diaries, but the ones we have seen don't account for those five missing years. The folks at Oakdale have looked repeatedly, with no result. Anyone having any ideas about where the missing diaries might be is asked to please get in touch.

Well, for now let's forget what we don't have and consider what we do, because it is the work of a man who put first things first. The first entry taken from the diary states, "I left home for Jamestown, N.C. June 21st, 1865 and arrived at Logan Factory Sunday June 25th 1865. Commenced business on Monday morning June 26th, 1865. Logan Factory, Jamestown, N.C."

Home for Cook was in Isle of Wight County, Virginia. And that is where the machinery for Logan Factory had been purchased from Scott's Mill before hostilities began in 1861. The war sidelined the spinning mill, and the mill machinery was stored at Danville while owners of the mill used the site for gun making during the war. Gun manufacturing ceased at the end of 1864, however, and C.P. Mendenhall, Ezekial P. Jones and Nathan Gardner prepared to move the machinery south as soon as possible.

Cook's diary records those first days at "the factory" on the banks of Deep River, a short distance away from the North Carolina Railroad. Many entries began with the weather: "Fine weather," "Rained very hard last night" or "Quite warm." Business usually came next: how many bales purchased and from whom, how many "bunches" produced and what expenditures were made and for what. He often went to Greensboro or High Point, and he often tells whom he met and where and what business was conducted.

When water was low, production was down. Cook noted on July 27, 1865: "Never have run half of the machinery here yet. Have not got the power to drive it."

On the other hand, when the water was high, there were different problems, as he noted four days later: "Rained very hard last night water quite high…Several hands out today in consequence of the rain and high water. They could not get over the bridge, the water being over it. Most of the hands do not live on the place as there is no houses for them to live in." In September he complained that "Leadbetter run the grist mill last night until mid night, which causes us to have to stop today."

Cook was fifty-two. He had been an officer in the Army of Northern Virginia. He mentioned the boardinghouse where he lived and made reference to going "up to the depot," so I believe he lived nearer to the factory. He makes careful note of when he mailed letters to his wife. On Sundays, he attended services in various places, one being at the "school house near the depot [Flint Hill,

Thomas Cook, a Virginian and former Confederate officer, installed the cotton mill machinery in 1865 for what became Oakdale Cotton Mill. He was the mill's superintendent until his death in 1889. *Courtesy Historic Jamestown Society.*

probably]"; Rev. Mr. Dalton, Presbyterian, "preaches there the first Sunday in every month." He also attended "meeting" in High Point and went to the Monthly Meeting at Deep River at least once. Eventually, he and his wife and daughter became members of the Methodist Episcopal Church.

The Mendenhall, Jones and Gardner company was disposing of stores, machinery and assorted items used in gun making but no longer needed for cotton spinning. There is a good bit of information on business practices of the period, and it is obvious that cash money was in short supply.

In late September, Cook visited his family in Isle of Wight but returned to Jamestown alone, and his family did not join him until about 1866, according to family records. He and his wife, Mary J., had six children—John, Thomas, Lucy, James, William and Robert—all of whom moved to Jamestown, though James went on to Texas.

Cook spent his remaining years as superintendent of the cotton factory, which at the time of his death in 1889 was called the Oakdale Cotton Factory. He had been a widower for many years. His wife died in 1873 and they both were buried at Deep River Friends, as were several of their children and grandchildren.

When Joseph S. Ragsdale wrote Cook's obituary in 1889, he mentioned Cook's "sweet cheerful spirit," adding that he enjoyed life and was "happiest when he was busiest."

He did stay busy. Certainly, in the twenty-three years that he spent at Oakdale, Thomas H. Cook constructed a strong foundation for a business that has had a very good run.

Joseph S. Ragsdale

A Trinity College report of May 21, 1859, on the grades and deportment of Joseph Sinclair Ragsdale shows he did extremely well, receiving 100 in Latin and English literature, 99 in Greek and 98 in algebra and composition. He also received a 1 in Distinction (for grades), and a 1 in Honor (for "scholarship, attention to duty and moral character").

Joseph S. Ragsdale is remembered in Jamestown as the first in a long line of Ragsdales to be associated with Oakdale Cotton Mill, followed in line by William Gannaway, William G. Jr., Thomas Cook, Thomas C. Jr and the present head of the company, William G. III, widely known as "Billy."

The Trinity College report is printed on very thin paper and probably has been folded for nearly 150 years, but it has been well cared for. The written grades are at the top of the sheet, and the bottom is an explanation of the

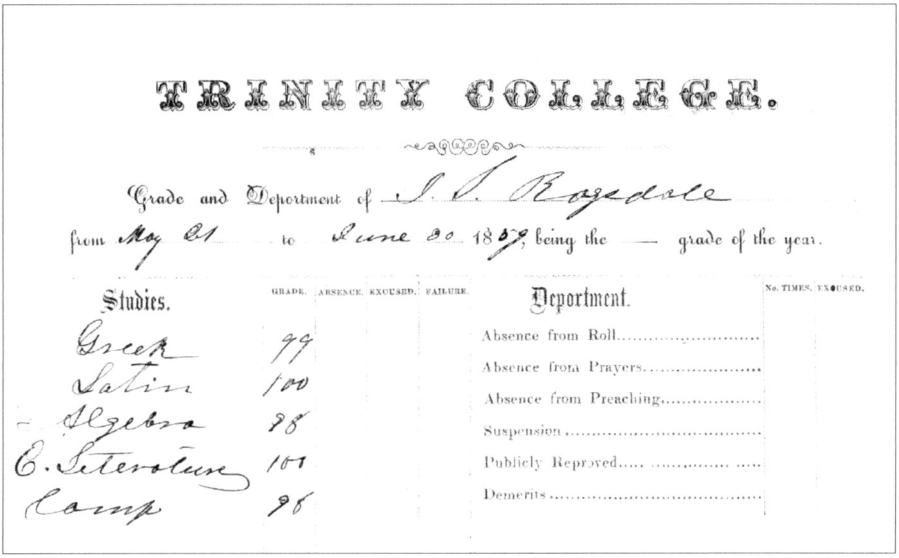

TRINITY COLLEGE.

Grade and Deportment of J. S. Ragsdale
from May 21 to June 30 1879, being the — grade of the year.

Studies.	Grade.	Absence.	Excused.	Failure.
Greek	99			
Latin	100			
Algebra	98			
E. Literature	101			
Comp	96			

Deportment.	No. Times.	Excused.
Absence from Roll		
Absence from Prayers		
Absence from Preaching		
Suspension		
Publicly Reproved		
Demerits		

Trinity College report for Joseph S. Ragsdale. Trinity College later moved from its Randolph County, North Carolina home to Durham, North Carolina, where it soon became Duke University. *Courtesy Historic Jamestown Society.*

grading and then a brief paragraph on fees and schedules. "B. Craven, President," is printed at the bottom. There's a handwritten note on the back that says, "Look round and bring us a number of boys from Old Guilford."

That note was surely written by Braxton Craven himself, a tireless promoter of his college in the Randolph County community that grew up around it. Trinity, like most of the Piedmont's small colleges and academies, always teetered on the brink of financial disaster but offered a good classical education.

The report is among items given to the Historic Jamestown Society by John Ragsdale, a great-grandson of the former Trinity student. These items were donated because of the connection between the Ragsdale family and the Oakdale Mill Project that has been undertaken by the society.

Also given was the historically significant "Minute Book of the Oakdale Manufacturing Company of Greensboro N.C. Organized October 1st 1873. Charter granted October 8th 1873." Handwritten minutes of meetings of stockholders and directors until October 1892 are on lined pages between the marbled covers of this old record book.

A third item is also of great interest: "History of Jamestown, North Carolina," by Virginia Ragsdale, a senior thesis she wrote as a history student at Guilford College in 1929. Virginia was a daughter of Joseph S. Ragsdale.

Both the school report and the record book are representative of J.S. Ragsdale's younger years, beginning in 1859, with his first of three years at Trinity College. About midway through the nineteen years covered by the minute book, by 1884, Ragsdale had been hired by Oakdale's then owner, Marshall Phillips, to manage the mill's business and financial affairs. He was forty-eight years old.

In the interim, Ragsdale had completed college and had purchased in 1862 the old Flint Hill schoolhouse in Jamestown from his cousin, John Freeman.

In 1863, he enlisted in the Confederate army and served as a first lieutenant in Company F, Fifty-fourth Regiment, North Carolina Infantry. He was taken prisoner in September 1864. Files at Oakdale Cotton Mill hold copies of letters he wrote home to family members during his service, and they are long, legible, carefully phrased, informative and affectionate.

When the war was over, he returned to Jamestown, met Emily Idol at E.E. Pitts's writing school in Old Jamestown and married her soon afterward. He taught at his school and partnered with his brother, John R. Ragsdale, in a nursery business operating in Pleasant Garden.

He worked briefly at the Silver Hill Mine in Davidson County and also for the J. Van Lindley nursery.

An essay by Virginia Ragsdale on those years, "Our Early Home and Childhood," portrays a happy and busy but frugal home life in the six-room house. Water was carried from a spring, where the family washing was done and perishable foods were kept. There was at least one bed in every room. Meals were simple. There were four children, the first of whom died as an infant. A small inheritance of Emily's was used to purchase twelve acres, "the beginning of what Father habitually called our 'sweet and happy home,'" as Virginia wrote.

Another glimpse of the younger days of Ragsdale shows him active in the Methodist Sunday school. In 1873, he was the Sunday school superintendent for the local Methodist congregation, while Thomas Cook was secretary and treasurer of the same group. Thomas Cook was the man who guided the fortunes of "the factory" that became Oakdale from 1865 until his death in 1889.

So Cook had a good chance to observe the younger man and was probably responsible for drawing him into the position at Oakdale in 1884 that would occupy the rest of his life.

The artifacts representing Ragsdale's life in Jamestown are welcome, indeed, and will be carefully tended by the Historic Jamestown Society.

Filming for the Oakdale Mill Project

The one week spent filming interviews and local scenery for the Oakdale Mill Project felt like at least a dozen forty-eight-hour days, and each hour was different from the one before. It was a grand experience.

It actually took place on six consecutive days in July 2007, the culmination of our attempt to record on film a history of Oakdale Cotton Mill, its employees and its mill village.

Filming was in the capable hands of a three-man professional crew from California, a group that filmmaker Mary Dalton had worked with before. Overall planning had been going on for months, as Dalton did what needed doing, most of which is still as mysterious to me now as it was before.

All of Jamestown was the set, but two rooms generously made available by Jamestown United Methodist Church were used for most of the interviews. Twenty-nine people were interviewed on camera, talking with Pat Koehler, Mary Dalton or myself.

About half the working time was spent in and near Oakdale Cotton Mill, filming machinery and equipment while listening to the plant manager describe the various parts of the manufacturing process. A few employees demonstrated their jobs as they worked. We watched as a batch of yarn was dyed to match a manufacturer's order, a noisy process in a hot room with a wet floor, accomplished with skill and aplomb by the experienced operator.

The mill's exterior was recorded on film, too, from all directions except up. Close up, nearby and from across the river, every angle possible was explored. Inside the mill, bricked-in windows in some walls show the size of earlier buildings and where newer additions enlarged the floor space of the mill as it increased its size, output and number of employees. One early room housed the old water wheel, which is now at the bottom of the river, too heavy to salvage.

Some of Jamestown's oldest houses are in the mill village neighborhood, also known as "the holler." We know from old photos that some of those houses nearest the mill itself date from the 1880s. Many of them show age and neglect, while others look solid and comfortable. One householder told us that her place very near the river was her "little bit of heaven," and it was indeed peaceful and homey.

Pat Koehler was the principal interviewer. She set up the schedule with those who had offered to be filmed, making notes from the project surveys, and in some cases from earlier interviews, to supply questions for each person. This involved keeping an incredible amount of information in her head so that it all went smoothly.

The milldam and Oakdale Cotton Mill were photographed on a quiet early August morning in 2007 during the mill project filming. *Courtesy Historic Jamestown Society.*

Most interviews began on a tentative note, but nearly everyone relaxed as things went along, and most enjoyed telling their stories.

Loyalty has probably been the most important element in the relationship of the mill village residents with each other, and with the mill. And it has worked both ways, with employees counting on good advice and a helping hand being available to them from the mill owners. "One big happy family" was heard again and again.

After some time is spent editing extraneous materials from the recordings, these interviews will be preserved. A half-hour-long DVD, polished, edited and with snippets of interviews mixed with background film and some use of still photographs, will be available soon. The filmmaker's art and craftsmanship will produce that half hour. I can't wait to see it.

Part VI

Bad Times Leave Their Stories Behind

Wars, epidemics and accidents are always part of the recollected past. Here are some examples.

Tragedy on a Sunday Evening

Ever since tracks for the North Carolina Railroad were first laid to run east and west (more or less) just south of Jamestown in the 1850s, the community has seen its share of accidents along those shiny rails.

At least two of these happened on Sunday evenings, which were especially busy times for the trains. As you or I get into the car or bus and go to church, theatre, shopping, friends' homes or whatnot, our counterparts in the old days climbed aboard the train to go a few miles and do many of the same things. The trains were frequent, the depots were relatively clean and comfortable, the final destinations easily reached by foot or trolley and plenty of familiar faces were on the coaches. On Sunday nights, lots of people were returning home or going elsewhere for the workweek ahead.

A man named Wil Odel broke a leg and received a terrible gash on his head when he and several others jumped off the train from Charlotte as it passed Jamestown on Sunday night, June 20, 1880. Three days later, when the Greensboro *Patriot* published a notice of the event, he was still at Jamestown in critical condition, not expected to live. The 1880 census shows a young man by that name boarding with a local family, so he was probably returning home.

Grim as that was for Mr. Odel and his loved ones, another local accident occurring some years later was far worse. It also happened on a Sunday, on March 19, 1916, and resulted in at least one death, three critical injuries and numerous others ranging in severity from great to slight.

This steam engine on display with a tender and one car at the North Carolina Transportation Museum at Spencer, North Carolina, is similar in age and style to the one that wrecked in Jamestown in 1916. Spencer was the Southern Railway's steam locomotive repair facility, begun in 1896. *Courtesy of the author.*

The wreck of Southern passenger train No. 43 occurred at the small Jamestown station just after 7:00 p.m., caused by derailed freight cars crashing into the slowly moving passenger train. The train was under the supervision of longtime employee Arch Rowsie, who had recently received an award for his long service to the line. The conductor was W.L. Finks, and the freight engineer was E.C. Elmore.

The train, just in from Greensboro, was leaving the station and headed toward High Point and points beyond. The account in the High Point *Enterprise* said that as cars were jammed together, pieces of lumber were forced through the passenger coaches and a baggage car turned over.

The death, which occurred a few hours after the accident, was that of twenty-three-year-old Mrs. Hazel Hedgecock Hiatt of High Point. The critical injuries were to Miss Mary Green of Thomasville, P.H. Carroll of Oak Hill, Virginia, and Miss Caroline Biggers of Thomasville. Miss Ethel Johnson of Jamestown was among the severely injured, and was the only

Jamestown person listed in the account. Injuries to a long list of people included many serious lacerations, fractures and heavy bruises.

This was the Easter season, and several of the passengers had attended a presentation of the popular oratorio *The Holy City* at State Normal. One was on her way home from Guilford College. Others likely were businessmen getting an early start to the workweek. It wasn't unheard of for millworkers to board in one town during the week and return home on weekends.

The newspaper account of the wreck said that its exact cause might never be known, since it was neither a head-on collision nor a rear-end one. The impact was between freight cars derailed on a parallel track and a slowly moving train. However, it was known that Mrs. Hiatt was seated next to the window, and apparently the most severe injuries, as well as hers, were caused by lumber being forced through the window into the coach.

There were many willing hands nearby to help the passengers and later to clear the wreckage. Many people had come to meet arrivals and also, since the depot was a central part of the community, a lot of others came just to watch the trains.

The ones who did so on that particular night got a lot more than they bargained for. However, one, Miss Mary Green of Thomasville, whose left leg suffered a serious break, went on to a successful marriage, to S.R. Matthews, and a long teaching career, according to her son Roger Matthews. Although the accident left her with a crooked left leg, her overall health was good and she lived to the age of ninety-seven.

Two Bright Spots in the 1933 Freight Train Accident

The newspaper called it a ravine. It really is a ravine, of sorts, and in 1933 it probably seemed more rough and rugged than it does now. This is the sloping ground on both sides of the railroad track and Depot Street as the rail line runs roughly north from its crossing of Oakdale Road. The slope is steepest on the Main Street side, where business buildings stand at the crest.

In the ravine is where a Southern Railway freight train was derailed during the early morning hours of December 2, 1933. Fourteen cars bound for Washington lurched and toppled off the tracks less than two hundred yards beyond the depot, spilling coal, flour, furniture, railroad ties, lumber and more, plus their own splintered sides and frames, along the narrow right of way.

The freight was an unscheduled one, with John Sparger aboard as engineer. The derailment was thought to have been caused by what was referred to as a broken truck. However, no additional explanation was offered. We are left to assume that a truck stalled on or near the tracks and that Sparger's engine either hit it or tried to make a sudden stop to avoid it. The results were the same either way. It tied up both the northbound and the southbound tracks, because the wreckage was tossed over both sets of rails. The force of the wreck ploughed some rail sections up.

The overturned coal car spilled coal in a deep pile several yards long. How many aprons and shirttails were filled with the wonderful black stuff before the cleanup crews arrived? This was depression time; temptation to salvage would have been pretty strong.

It wasn't long before a crew estimated to be between fifty and seventy-five men arrived from Spencer and Greensboro to clear the wreckage. By noon, five of the cars had been cleared away from the tracks. One car splintered while the wrecker tried to remove it, and the force scattered railroad ties. However, the southbound track was reopened by mid-afternoon, and the northbound track was cleared and repaired by about 7:00 p.m.

In contrast to the 1916 passenger train wreck that occurred at about the same place, no one was killed or injured in this incident.

There was another bright spot in the 1933 affair, in that it provided a splendid daylong spectacle and diversion for those who had a few moments to spare, and more especially for those who had nothing else to do at all. There was a large spectator gallery on either side of the tracks all day long. Some folks were perched on the ravine slope behind houses and stores that line Main Street. Some were scattered along the hillside off of Oakdale Road, just watching.

A Stanley Family Story

One could hardly blame the Adolphus Stanley family for moving out of Jamestown. Dealing with Union raiders in the waning days of the Civil War was bad enough. But when returning Confederate veterans of the war brought smallpox home with them later, it was just too much. After Adolphus's wife Hannah died from the disease, the family left and before 1868 had settled in Henderson County, Illinois.

The Stanley family lived in a house that was at or near the northwest corner of Main (Federal) and Union Streets, the Richard Mendenhall store building being across Union Street to the east and the Richard Mendenhall

House being across Main Street to the south. The house had belonged to William Stanley—perhaps was built by him—and he and his wife Lydia Beard raised a family there. Among their children was Adolphus E., who continued to live in the old home following the death of his parents.

Stanley held the construction contract to build a woolen mill nearby in late 1861 and early 1862. It was owned by James Ruffin Mendenhall, George C. Mendenhall's son. The mill stood north of the old meetinghouse, near the bank of Deep River's South Fork. In present-day terms, it was just about where the children's playground is now in High Point City Lake Park. Young Mendenhall and his partner, Duncan A. McRae of Cheraw, South Carolina, had a contract with Major James Sloan, quartermaster at Greensboro, to manufacture gray cloth for Confederate uniforms. In April 1865, when General George Stoneman's raiders sought the location of the gun factory, which they intended to destroy, they were directed to the woolen mill, which they seized and burned. The workers at the mill were temporarily detained by the raiders at the Stanley home. The gun factory, located at the present site of Oakdale Cotton Mill, escaped untouched.

For some reason, after Adolphus had moved away with his children, a story circulated among neighbors that Hannah Stanley, overwhelmed by a large family of small children and bad health, had "jumped into the well, and thereby ended her troubles of this world." Then, the story went, Adolphus's sister Rebecca came to help care for the family but, after peeking at the deceased Hannah to satisfy her curiosity, "got the smallpox and died."

In Illinois, other stories from the family itself dispute those. Hannah died of smallpox, according to her descendants, and Adolphus was left alone because everyone was afraid of the disease. Late on the day of the death, a man who had once worked for Adolphus in the mill came to the house with his wife, and they offered to prepare Hannah for burial. Both had survived smallpox and so were immune. They were humble people who would never have been invited guests in the Stanley home, but Adolphus was so grateful to them that he often reminded his children that "one never knows upon whom one may have to depend for help."

Sister Rebecca, who was the widow of G.W. Causey, did not die of smallpox, but moved to Illinois with her brother and died there many years later. Adolphus remarried and had seven more children. He is buried in the cemetery at Raritan, Illinois.

One more story is told by the Illinois descendants, this one about the Stoneman raid. It recounts that Adolphus was taken from his office at gunpoint and backed up against a wall while the soldiers set fire to the mill. Years later, in Illinois, a salesman stopped at the Stanley home and asked if he and his horse could stay the night because of a severe storm raging. Adolphus and his visitor spoke of the war, and the account of the woolen mill's burning was offered up as something of interest. The visitor later told Mrs. Stanley that he had been the Union soldier who had held a gun on Adolphus, but didn't want to admit his part in the raid to "the old gentleman."

The Illinois stories came from a Stanley descendant, Ruth D. Frisk, and were published in the *Guilford Genealogist* (number. fifty-one).

Where Jefferson Davis Slept

Stories pop up, and you don't know how seriously to take them because you don't know where they came from. One such story is the one that links Jamestown with Jefferson Davis, president of the Confederacy, in his flight from Richmond in late April 1865. I've looked high and low for its source, but then I stumbled over it accidentally in an old issue of the *Guilford Genealogist*, published by the Guilford County Genealogical Society. That issue is the journal's number thirteen, Winter 1981, in case you want to look it up at the library. It reprints an article from the High Point *Enterprise* of May 1, 1924, and adds some related information.

The article is based on an account given by the eldest daughter of Dr. Shubal G. Coffin, written up by her daughter and then signed by the originator on February 2, 1923, and published (after her death) by the *Enterprise*. She was Mary Roxanna Coffin, and she first married T.D. Harris and, later, George Gregory, a Greensboro attorney.

The account sets the gloomy scene—the war's end, the impoverished Southern army waiting to be dismissed, the procession of dilapidated vehicles and poor horses that carried the Davis household southwest from Greensboro, where no suitable place could be found to spend the night.

The pertinent paragraph says, "Jefferson Davis rode a horse which gave out about three miles from Greensboro, south, near John Hiatt's, who entertained him that night. The next morning he gave him a clay-bank horse, which he rode off. As he passed the house of Dr. Coffin he was joined by his secretary, Mr. Traniam, who had spent the night there."

According to Rice University's Jefferson Davis Chronology website, that would have been the night of April 15, 1865.

In that same issue, the *Guilford Genealogist* also published a letter written on May 22, 1865, by John Hiatt to his sons Philander and Thomas. It does not mention Mr. Davis, but does say that the Confederates, all Johnson's army, camped on his land for nine days, ruining the wheat and oat crop on all but 10 or 12 out of his 160 acres. He begged his boys to come home.

In addition, a letter from Wyatt Jackson Armfield, written in 1921, speaks of the Davis party, after it was unable to find accommodation for about two hundred men on horseback in Greensboro, coming "over the old Salisbury stage-road 5 miles west of Greensboro to the home of Mr. John Hiatt, who was a large land-owner and slave-holder, and were entertained there for the night."

He continued:

> *I saw this cavalcade as it passed through Jamestown, N.C. about 10 o'clock the following morning, which was Sunday, and it was a very impressive sight, for the horses were fine and well-groomed, the ambulances looked new and shining, and formed a strong contrast to the poor, half-starved horses and equipment of the Confederate soldiers, to which we were accustomed. A few days afterward he and party were captured near Washington, Ga., and Mr. Davis was afterward imprisoned for some time at Fort Monroe, Va.*

There are plenty of Jamestown associations in those accounts. Wyatt Armfield was a prominent citizen who might best be remembered now for his handsome residence, Sapona Side, formerly located on Deep River Road. Mrs. Gregory's daughter, who wrote down the account dictated by her mother, was identified as Mrs. Dan Moore; she was Jennie M. Harris, who married Daniel W. Moore.

Where was the John Hiatt farm? I don't know. I hope someone will enlighten me.

New Information on Coffin's Guest

The previous section told of a statement made in 1923 by Mary Roxanna Coffin Gregory that said Jefferson Davis's "secretary," a "Mr. Traniam," had spent the night of April 15, 1865, at the home of her father, Dr. Shubal G. Coffin, near the depot in the new section of Jamestown that had grown up near the railroad.

The section also reported on information saying Davis had spent that night at the farm of John Hiatt, said to be three miles west of Greensboro, but the exact location not known.

Here are some updates.

Davis, of course, was president of the Confederacy and at that time was traveling south from Richmond with a sizable entourage of household staff and Confederate government officials.

At Greensboro, the party abandoned the train because of burned railroad bridges ahead, and managed to gather up a convoy of ambulances and wagons to accompany those who set out on horseback. They failed to find accommodations in Greensboro (a story in itself), and had no choice but to continue on toward Salisbury.

Leaving Greensboro behind, then, Davis and some members of his party were given shelter by a man named John Hiatt on his farm, which was about three miles west of the city.

Soon after that column was published, Boyd Lamberth of Reidsville got in touch and provided more detailed information about the location of the John Hiatt farm. According to his research, the farm lay along what is now Green Point Road, just east of Merrit Drive in Greensboro. Green Point parallels High Point Road and is about a block north of it.

The Guilford County map made in 1908 by engineer C.M. Miller shows T.C. Hiatt owning property at that place where a road from Pomona (now Merritt Drive) joined the main road between Greensboro and High Point.

So it all makes sense. The Davis party was headed south, and this place was on the old Salisbury Stage Road leading to Charlotte and beyond. In 1865, the Greensboro city limits were far to the east, putting this farm several miles out into the country.

A little more investigation of the secretary, "Mr. Tranium," reported by Coffin's daughter, didn't find anyone with that name in any of the Davis biographies. However, a Mr. George A. Trenholm was secretary of the treasury, and was one of the members of the Confederate cabinet traveling south with Davis in April 1865.

He had severe neuralgia. In Greensboro, he was given temporary shelter at the John M. Morehead mansion. When he left, the Morehead family provided a mattress for his ambulance, or so says Michael B. Ballard in *A Long Shadow: Jefferson Davis and the Final Days of the Confederacy.*

It seems quite likely that Dr. Coffin would have taken in a man as sick as Trenholm apparently was. It also seems likely that it was George Trenholm who spent the night at Dr. Coffin's home on April 15, 1865.

Thanks to Mr. Lamberth for providing the information on the Hiatt farm.

Confederate Munitions Found in 1928

The North Carolina Department of Transportation is building a new bridge over Deep River on U.S. 29-A, otherwise known as the Greensboro–High Point Road, or West Main Street, in Jamestown. Well, no doubt you've noticed.

The last time they built a bridge here, they found six old bombs or shells in the muck several feet below the river bottom, where the center support of the previous bridge had rested. Two bombs were in a box stenciled "From Richmond Arsenal." These discoveries were made on November 4 and 5, 1926. And they were just the beginning.

The shells were of the old "cannon ball" type, with a hole in one side and a fuse running through a wooden plug. They were filled with powder and grapeshot. They were the kind of cannonballs familiar to cartoon-watchers—with a lit fuse throwing off sparks and making a "ssst" noise. It seemed obvious the bombs were of Civil War vintage. The boxes were of inch-thick pine plank, soft and rotten.

The shells were in good condition, just slightly corroded. Laborers of the F.D. Lewis & Son Company, sinking a coffer dame where a pier would be placed in the middle of the river, were excited, expecting to find gold or cannons or bleached bones or who knew what.

Foreman J.T. Brosius and his crew dragged out a box after a pick caught its corner about five feet below the bed of the stream. The box contained two shells. A third one was found outside the box. The next day, three more were found in another box with a space for another shell. The discovery was reported on November 6 and 7 in the High Point *Enterprise*, and on November 7 in the Greensboro *Daily News*.

Lewis & Son officials reportedly took both boxes to Mrs. Hiram Bell, the president of the Greensboro Historical Museum Association. The *Daily News* said they would be on display in the public library building and kept "in the museum quarters" there.

After several months, Charles Ross, an assistant attorney general assigned to the Highway Commission, made an official announcement of the discoveries, and they were publicized in the *News & Observer* of Raleigh on March 30, 1927. By then, the list of discoveries had grown to include shells of various sizes, muskets with rotten stocks and rusty barrels, sabers and scabbards, ammunition and "old fashioned weapons."

The High Point *Enterprise* reported the finds were stacked around the office walls of John Williamson Mills, the chief engineer for the Fifth District, and the office looked like a "museum of Confederate implements of warfare."

Nearly everything was damaged, probably deliberately to make it useless. No one doubted the items were of Confederate origin. An unidentified Confederate veteran said he thought there were many more relics embedded under the river.

As laborers did their work, various theories were advanced to explain when, why and how the stuff had come to be dumped into Deep River at that place.

One idea was that a Confederate detachment dropped the stuff while fording the river. Henry Clag Briggs pretty quickly disputed this in a 1926 letter to the editor of the *Enterprise*. Briggs's familiarity with the location allowed him to state with authority that there had never been a ford there because "there has always been a rocky cliff on the west side of the river."

There is indeed a rocky cliff there. The distance between the bridge and river is quite visible now, with the bridge halfway demolished, but it was not noticeable before. It was easy to drive west from the Jamestown Library to High Point City Lake Park and not realize that you had crossed a bridge; that the bridge was, well, maybe sixty feet above a river; and that the west end of the bridge was perched on the rocky cliff.

The *Daily News* published information from A.M. Gunn of Sanford, who had it from Charles T. Wall of Rural Hall. The news clipping isn't dated but apparently comes from the same 1926–27 period. Wall, a Confederate teamster, had told Gunn of being ordered during the last days of the conflict to get a wagonload of munitions stores out of the reach of Federal forces. So Wall loaded up a two-horse wagon, drove it to the bridge over Deep River at Jamestown and dumped the munitions in the river.

I found a Charles T. Wall, in "North Carolina Confederate Veterans Grave Locations," buried at Nazareth Lutheran Church in Rural Hall. He served in Company G, Twenty-first Regiment, North Carolina Troops, the Town Fork Invincibles, from Forsyth County. He was a sergeant, wounded at Gettysburg, taken prisoner, exchanged and continued to serve, but has no record after February 1865. He died in 1908.

According to H.C. Briggs's letter, a covered bridge built before the Civil War was used until it was washed away "in the spring of the surrender" (1865).

Briggs, in 1926, offers:

> *There were many of those shells scattered around Jamestown...Soon after the war the older boys collected a lot of shells and built a log heap of them*

> *where Mr. Will Ragsdale's house now stands, set fire to it and blew shells and rocks all over the woods.*

But what happened to the ones dug up in 1926?

Munitions Mystery Solved

The mystery of the Confederate munitions is solved, thanks to a phone call from Ken Norman, a retired High Point fireman.

Readers will recall the previous section that reported on the bombs and shells found buried in Deep River in Jamestown. Everyone concluded that the munitions were of Civil War vintage. By the time construction of the bridge was completed, a fairly large store of these items had been collected.

That collection apparently was held in the office of John Williamson Mills, the chief engineer for the state highway department's Fifth District, and that office, according to the High Point *Enterprise*, looked like a "museum of Confederate implements of warfare."

What happened to all that stuff?

Well, as often happens, a reader came to the rescue with information. This time it was Ken Norman telling me where to find the next installment of this saga.

This one, also from the *Enterprise*, is dated August 13, 1928, and reported that during the coming week a number of old cannonballs unearthed during the Jamestown bridge construction would be exploded to "discover the durability of gunpowder." An ordnance officer from Fort Bragg in Fayetteville would conduct the test. He would come to High Point just for this purpose.

The test was to take place on the Motsinger Farm, which is now on the Old Winston Road. The day had not yet been set, or at least was not announced, which was probably a wise move.

Among items to be exploded were two eighty-pound balls, one twelve-pound ball and six or eight smaller ones. The test would establish whether the explosives were as effective today as they would have been during the Civil War when they were manufactured.

Ken pointed out during our conversation that old gunpowder is very unstable. As a retired fireman, he is probably more aware of those dangers than most. However, anyone scouring old battlefields or military campsites for relics should keep that in mind.

SELECTED BIBLIOGRAPHY

In addition to various books, newspapers and periodicals cited within the text, the following were also used as sources:

Browning, Mary A. *Bending the Twigs in Jamestown: A History of Education in Jamestown, North Carolina, 1755–1945.* Jamestown, NC: Historic Jamestown Society, 2004.

———. *Historical Places In & Around Jamestown, N.C.* Jamestown, NC: self-published, 2008.

Guilford County, NC, Records of Deeds.

———, Records of Wills.

Hinshaw, William Wade. *Encyclopedia of American Quaker Genealogy, Vol. I North Carolina.* Baltimore: Genealogical Publishing Company, 1969.

Mendenhall Papers, various, Friends Historical Collection, Guilford College, Greensboro, NC.

Oakdale Mill Project Papers, Historic Jamestown Society, Jamestown, NC.

Ragsdale Papers, Jamestown Alumni Archives, Jamestown Public Library, Jamestown, NC.

INDEX